REVELATION
All Things New

AN EIGHT-WEEK STUDY WITH
Dr. Tony W. Cartledge

THE *Nurturing*
FAITH™
BIBLE STUDY SERIES

© 2016
Published in the United States by Nurturing Faith Inc., Macon GA,
www.nurturingfaith.net.

Library of Congress Cataloging-in-Publication Data is available.

ISBN 978-1-938514-96-8

*Unless otherwise indicated, scripture quotations are taken from
the New Revised Version of the Bible.*

Cover photo by Tony W. Cartledge

A colonnade from the city of Laodicea, known in Revelation
as a wealthy city whose church had grown lukewarm.

Interior and cover design by Amy C. Cook

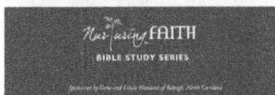

Other resources from
Nurturing Faith
BOOKS

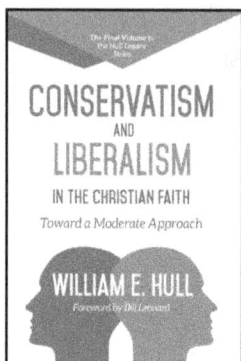

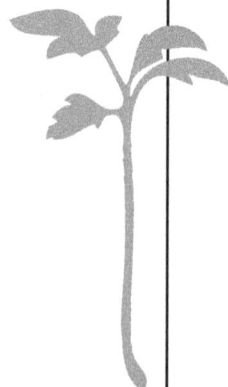

CONTENTS

ABBREVIATIONS

ESV   English Standard Version

KJV   King James Version

HCSB   Holman Christian Standard Bible

NET   New English Translation (also known as the NETBible)

LXX   Septuagint, an early Greek translation of the Old Testament

MT   Masoretic Text, the "standard" Hebrew text of the Old Testament

NASB   New American Standard Bible, 1977 edition

NAS95   New American Standard Bible, 1995 edition

NIV   New International Version, 1984 edition

NIV11   New International Version, 2011 edition

NRSV   New Revised Standard Version

PREFACE

Bible study is a discipline that calls for the engagement of both hearts and minds. The Nurturing Faith Bible Series focuses on biblical texts that with careful study and divine guidance can expand the mind and enrich the heart.

Dr. Tony Cartledge brings the insights of a scholar, the heart of a pastor, and the communication skills of a seasoned writer and editor to this important task. With superb scholarship he guides learners to a clearer understanding of the context—language, culture, and setting—in which the biblical accounts occurred.

Then the important question is considered, "How do these ancient words speak to us as people of faith today?" Truth—not bound by time and culture—awaits those who are willing to dig, contemplate, and apply these biblical treasures.

Respecting the need to engage scripture with both heart and mind, there is no attempt to "dumb down" the lessons or to ignore the challenges of serious inquiry. This is a distinguishing mark of the Nurturing Faith Bible Study Series

Therefore, each lesson concludes with "The Hardest Question" in which Dr. Cartledge both raises and responds to such challenges in understanding and applying the biblical revelation to today's living.

An honest wrangling with the biblical texts—while guided by God's Spirit—produces clearer understanding and stronger commitments. Such Bible study will indeed nurture one's faith.

This thoughtful approach is especially important when studying the often misconstrued and challenging final book of the Bible, known as the book of Revelation. This apocalyptic writing has been the source of many dramatic and failed predictions. Its obscure language has led many people either to ignore the strange book or use its imagery for unintended purposes.

In these excellent studies, however, Dr. Cartledge explores the historical and cultural setting in which the dramatic revelation was given and provides keen insights into the timeless message that still flows from the ancient texts.

Those who engage in these insightful lessons will be encouraged to live more faithfully with the promised hope that, in Christ, all things are made new.

What does Revelation really mean? Dig into these eight sessions to find out.

—John D. Pierce, Publisher
Nurturing Faith, Inc.

This volume in the Nurturing Faith Bible Study Series
is made possible through a generous gift from
Gene and Linda Pleasants of Raleigh, North Carolina

***

Nurturing Faith seeks sponsors for future volumes in this Bible study series.
To inquire, please contact office@nurturingfaith.net.

INTRODUCTION

The book of Revelation has fascinated the curious and frightened the timid while puzzling interpreters and challenging preachers for nearly two millennia. Also known as the Apocalypse of John, the ancient collection of visions has been the subject of intense scrutiny by Bible lovers of every stripe, but no one can claim to understand it fully. Much of the book was written in code-like metaphors, mainly to a group of insiders who would have understood its arcane symbolism. In most cases we can make educated guesses at what the author intended, but can hardly claim to have certain knowledge of every nuance.

While certainty is elusive and John's strange imagery may be offensive, the book of Revelation remains worthy of study. It comes to us as scripture believed to have been inspired by God—and if God has a word for us, we don't want to miss it.

The Genre

Reading Revelation insightfully requires care, because it is unlike most of the other New Testament writings: it belongs to a genre of literature called "apocalyptic," and it must be understood as such. Apocalyptic writings are a particular type of "crisis literature" that emerged during desperate times when traditional beliefs ran afoul of present reality and a new worldview was needed to make sense of life. Apocalyptic writings were especially popular in the last two centuries before Christ and the first two centuries after his birth—a tumultuous period of religious and political upheaval in which both Jews and Christians faced drastic threats to survival.

Revelation, by the author's own testimony, is an apocalypse. As such, it shares several characteristic features with other apocalyptic writings. These include an eschatological theology that believes the wicked will be judged and the righteous rewarded, a heavy dependence on symbolism, the use of numerology as a sort of code language, and some variation on a heavenly journey in which an angelic guide takes the writer on a visionary tour of things to come. All of these are found in Revelation.

When one has always believed that God is both all-powerful and always concerned for God's people—but the horrifying situation on the ground leads one to think God has gone missing—the one hopeful explanation is that God must be working behind the scenes to bring the present age crashing to an end in preparation for a new age in which enemies will be vanquished and those who currently suffer will be vindicated. That is the impetus for apocalyptic.

The latter half of Daniel is an Old Testament example. That author adopted the guise of a traditional Jewish hero from the sixth century Babylonian exile, but he actually wrote around 165 BCE during a time of intense persecution under the Seleucid rule of Antiochus IV Epiphanes, famed for his cruelty. The pagan king had sought to eliminate Judaism within his realm, which roughly coincided with the former kingdoms of Israel and Judah, including Jerusalem. As a provocation, he offered a sow on the altar of the temple and demanded that Jewish priests eat from it or die (this is probably what was meant by the "abomination of desolation" (9:27, 11:31, 12:1).

Many Jews were tortured and/or murdered, and for faithful Hebrews it seemed that the only hope was to look to a future age when God would defeat the evil rulers of the world, deliver the Jews, and introduce a new age of peace. The author's intention in Daniel 7-12 was to encourage his suffering compatriots through a document proclaiming that Daniel had foreseen the unfolding of history many years before. Daniel's apocalyptic visions included a "forecast" of the dynastic changes leading to the Jews' current plight, along with predictions of a glorious future in a new age that was just around the corner, reserved for those who persevered.

Similar apocalyptic writings were common during periods of severe trial. Isaiah 24-27, Ezekiel 38-39, and Zechariah 9-14, along with a few shorter texts, have apocalyptic characteristics. More than a dozen other writings, such as the *Apocalypse of Adam*, the *Apocalypse of Abraham*, and the *Apocalypse of Elijah* were known, but not accepted as part of the Old Testament canon.

Most apocalyptic writings, like Daniel, were written in the name of a Jewish hero who had lived many years before, and in such a way that the putative author had accurately predicted the current state of life through visions that typically included dueling spiritual powers, allegorical beasts symbolizing earthly kingdoms, the end of the present age, and a wonderful new age for the faithful.

An apocalyptic worldview permeates much of the New Testament, including some of the teachings attributed to Jesus. During times of hardship or persecution against the early church, writers from various Christian sects adopted the form of the apocalypse to "forecast" the present and to predict better days. Most of these writings did not make it into scripture, though many are known, including apocalypses claiming to have been written by Peter, Paul, James, Thomas, and others. Mark 13 and its parallels in Matthew 24 and Luke 21 have apocalyptic tendencies, but Revelation is the only full-blown apocalypse found in the New Testament.

John's Apocalypse was apparently written during a time of severe trial, probably during the last three decades of the first century, and circulated among the
churches in the western part of the Roman province of Asia, known today as Turkey. It fits neatly into the apocalyptic pattern with the exceptions that its author
does not write in the name of a former hero of the faith, but identifies himself as a
man named John, and he encloses his apocalypse within the framework of a letter.

The Author

Though he mentions his own name four times (1:1, 4, 9; 22:8), the author does
not identify himself further. We know of several early believers named John.
Which one was he? Or was he someone not otherwise mentioned in the New
Testament?

Writers as early as Justin Martyr (155 CE) identified the author as John the
son of Zebedee, one of Jesus' 12 apostles and the only one, according to church
tradition, to die a natural death. This view was challenged early on due to differences in language and style between Revelation and other books traditionally
attributed to John. There is also a problem in that the author speaks of the 12
apostles as having their names written on the foundations of the new Jerusalem
(21:14), which gives the impression that he is speaking of honored saints. It seems
odd that the author would have
written this way about himself. Similarly, if the author was
John, the beloved disciple, it is
surprising that he would not
have mentioned his personal
connection to Jesus.

Some early church fathers
identified the writer as someone
known as "John the Elder," who
was also associated by some
early writers with the letters
of 1-3 John. The author does
not use that title or any other,
however, simply calling himself John.

The Island of Patmos, where John reportedly wrote
the book of Revelation. Local tradition holds that he
did so in a cave now covered by a small monastery.

Noting the lack of other identification, Bruce Metzger suggests that John
the apostle is as good a guess as any: "it is probable that he intends his readers to
understand that he is the John who was so well known that he needed no other
titles or credentials"[1]

Most contemporary scholars are more hesitant to make the attribution. They
note many linguistic and thematic differences between the Gospel of John, the

letters of 1-3 John, and the book of Revelation. The author, then, could have been an early church leader who was well known in his own time and region, but otherwise unknown to us. Whoever the author was, he clearly considered himself to be a Christian prophet (1:3) and was well known to the churches of Asia Minor, for whom the book was written.[2] We may also assume that the author must have been known to the Romans and outspoken in his criticism of Roman rule, resulting in his exile on the Mediterranean island of Patmos, off the eastern coast of Asia Minor (1:9).

The Date

Some writers believe that Revelation reflects some of the persecutions that took place under Emperor Nero, who ruled from 54-68 CE, but his cruelty was mainly limited to believers in Rome. Even so, Nero was thought of as the archetype of a cruel Roman ruler, and is likely to have been in John's mind when he spoke of an "antichrist" identified by the code number 666. The numeric value of a Hebrew spelling of Nero's name adds up to that number, and a popular myth believed that Nero would rise again.

The first emperor known to require empire-wide worship was Domitian, who demanded that others address him as "our lord and god," something Christians could not do. Domitian's rule stretched from 81-96 CE. Thus, many scholars believe Revelation was most likely written in the mid-90s CE, near the end of Domitian's reign. Some later church fathers wrote of terrible atrocities against Christians that took place under Domitian's rule, though hard evidence for such persecution is scanty. Even when the imperial cult was in place, officially requiring all persons to acknowledge the divinity of the emperor, enforcement of the law was probably sporadic and scattered. We have no records of empire-wide oppression, though there is little doubt that localized persecutions took place at the whim of area officials.

Other evidence for a date near the end of the first century includes the statement in 2:8-11 that the church in Smyrna (modern Izmir) had suffered persecution for a long time. Polycarp (who served as bishop of Smyrna during the first half of the second century) wrote that the church did not exist until sometime in the 60s, after Paul's death, so the persecution must have occurred later.

Similarly, John describes the church in Laodicea as rich, but the city was virtually destroyed by an earthquake in 61 CE. It would probably have taken some years for the city, known for its banking industry, to rebuild and regain its reputation as a wealthy city.

The Audience

While clearly apocalyptic in nature, Revelation is cast in the form of a letter addressed to seven churches in the western part of the Roman province of Asia, now known as Turkey (1:4). The churches were in the cities of Ephesus, Smyrna, Pergamum, Thyatira, Sardis, Philadelphia, and Laodicea. A messenger beginning his journey in Ephesus could visit each of the churches by traveling

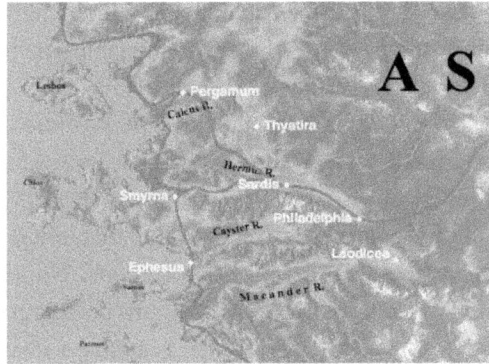

The "Seven Churches of Revelation" are in what is now western Turkey, called "Asia" in the New Testament. Note the island of Patmos at the lower left. Map courtesy of Accordance Bible Software.

north, then east, then south, following a roughly semi-circular route.

Although only the seven churches are named, it is likely that the Apocalypse would have been widely distributed among the churches in Asia and elsewhere. When received, the book was intended to be read aloud: "Blessed is the one who reads aloud the words of the prophecy, and blessed are those who hear and who keep what is written in it; for the time is near" (1:3). The book closes with a warning to "everyone who hears the words of the prophecy of this book," that they not add or subtract from it (22:18). Through the act of listening to the reading, hearers "entered into another universe and experienced a new reality."[3]

The Purpose

John's purpose in writing was twofold. On the one hand, he wanted to comfort beleaguered believers by focusing their attention on the second coming of Christ, which he apparently expected to happen in the near future. On the other hand, he sought to warn any who wavered of the danger of becoming too comfortable with Rome and its culture, calling compromisers to restore their faithfulness in Christ alone.

The book's structure is marked by a series of seven visions along with interpretive comments about the meaning of the visions. The first six visions (4:1-19:5) deal largely and repetitively with the "birth pangs" or "tribulations" thought to precede a shift from the old age to the coming new age. The final vision, played out in seven scenes, focuses on what John believed would come after: a new age in which God would create a new heaven and a new earth.

Although readers often assume that the visions should be read and interpreted chronologically, they are actually overlapping or even repetitive—

looking at the same realities through different images. Therefore, we should avoid approaching Revelation as a timetable for the last days, anticipating a carefully delineated sequence of events.

Similarly, we should not interpret the characters and events in Revelation in a literal fashion, but realize that most of the book, by John's own testimony, consists of visions. Such visions are typically characterized by abstract symbolism and word pictures, complex metaphors designed to convey truth without being an actual description of events. Numbers such as three, seven, and multiples of ten or twelve are important because of their symbolic meaning rather than numeric value. Strange beasts and mythical creatures appear to symbolize persons, nations, or spiritual realities, but we are not expected to believe that the fearsome seven-headed dragons or bizarre patchwork monsters have (or will have) a literal existence.

While much of Revelation is cryptic, and while we can't claim to understand it all, the book's focus on current suffering and future blessings provides a clear framework for John's call to avoid assimilation into an idolatrous culture and remain faithful to God. While we do not live under an emperor who claims to be god, there is much about our own culture that is idolatrous in the extreme. As a result, as strange as it might appear, the book offers much in the way of profit.

The lessons that follow are not designed as a comprehensive commentary on Revelation. Rather, they offer eight dips into the deep well of John's apocalypse, studies based on representative texts that highlight the primary focus of the book: hard times may come and evil may be strong, but God will prevail and the future for God's faithful people remains sure. For this we may be very grateful.

OUTLINE[4]

I. Prologue (1:1-8)
II. The "Son of Man" and his message to the churches (1:9–3:22)
III. Seven visions of shifting ages (4:1–22:5)
    A. God's throne room; opening the seven seals (4:1–8:5)
    B. Blowing the seven trumpets (8:6–11:19)
    C. The Roman Empire and Christian suffering (11:19–13:18)
    D. Seven angels of judgment (14:1-20)
    E. Seven bowls of wrath (15:1–16:21)
    F. The fall of "Babylon" (Rome) (17:1–19:5)
    G. Seven scenes of consummation: Christ's final triumph (19:6–22:5)
IV. Epilogue (22:6–21)

SELECTED RESOURCES FOR FURTHER STUDY

Ashcraft, Morris. "Revelation," in the *Broadman Bible Commentary*, Vol. 12. Nashville: Broadman Press, 1972.

Aune, David. *Revelation,* 3 vols. Word Biblical Commentary, Vols. 52a, 52b, 52c. Nashville: Thomas Nelson, 1997-98.

Boring, M. Eugene. *Revelation,* Interpretation: A Bible Commentary for Teaching and Preaching. Louisville, KY: John Knox, 1989.

Caird, G. B. *The Revelation of St. John the Divine.* New York: Harper & Row, 1966.

Metzger, Bruce. *Breaking the Code: Understanding the Book of Revelation.* Nashville: Abingdon Press, 1993.

Mounce, Robert H. *The Book of Revelation.* NICOT. Grand Rapids: Eerdmanns, 1977.

Reddish, Mitchell G. *Revelation.* Smyth & Helwys Bible Commentary. Macon, GA: Smyth & Helwys, 2001.

Talbert, Charles H. *The Apocalypse: A Reading of the Revelation of John.* Louisville, KY: Westminster John Knox, 1994.

NOTES

[1] Bruce Metzger, *Breaking the Code: Understanding the Book of Revelation* (Nashville: Abingdon Press, 1993), 14-15.

[2] See Mitchell G. Reddish, *Revelation,* Smyth & Helwys Commentary (Macon, GA: Smyth & Helwys, 2001), 17-19.

[3] Charles H. Talbert, *The Apocalypse: A Reading of the Apocalypse of John* (Louisville: Westminster John Knox, 1994), 4; citing David L. Barr, "The Apocalypse of John as Oral Enactment," *Interpretation* 40 (1986), 243-56.

[4] The outline on p. 6 is based largely on Talbert, *The Apocalypse,* 12.

Revelation 1:1-8

LOOK WHO'S COMING!

> *Look! He is coming with the clouds; every eye will see him . . .*
> *—Revelation 1:7a*

Do you love it or hate it—or just avoid it? The book of Revelation inspires all three responses. John's "apocalypse" was written to provide both challenge and encouragement to believers, but its message is shrouded in mystery and metaphors that leave it open to multiple (but not necessarily responsible) interpretations.

Revelation can't be read in the same way as other books of the New Testament. It is not a historical account, like the Gospels and Acts, or a personal letter, like the Epistles. Though framed by elements common to first-century letters: a greeting and blessing (1:4-6) followed by the main body of the letter (1:7–22:20) and a closing (22:21), the "body" of the letter is very different from other New Testament writings.

As noted in the introduction, the bulk of the Apocalypse belongs to a literary genre known as "apocalyptic," a particular type of literature that emerged during desperate times when traditional beliefs ran aground on the rocks of present reality and a new worldview was needed to make sense of life. When one believes that God is in control but sees little evidence of it, one possible explanation is that the world may be spiraling down, but God has something better in store—at least for believers.

Since they arise from times of persecution or crisis, apocalypses rely on metaphorical language and images that would be known to believers but not to their enemies. Unfortunately, sometimes they are also a mystery to modern readers. Even so, many readers have sought to interpret Revelation as a programmatic text designed to predict the end times in graphic detail. Combining numbers and symbols from the books of Daniel and Revelation, they seek to relate various

Writing with pictures: As Mitchell Reddish puts it, "To read and appreciate the book of Revelation, one must be aware of how the language and symbols of Revelation function ... the language of the book is primarily pictorial, symbolic language." The book's "evocative, powerful, emotive language" is often more like poetry than prose, and thus can be "mysterious and slippery."[1]

characters to the current day and predict a neat sequence of events leading up to a final world war centered in the Middle East (Armaggedon) and the resulting end of the age. ⛊

A popular view (but wrong): One of the most popular versions of this approach is called "premillennial dispensationalism." It was developed by J. N. Darby in the 19th century, popularized by C. I. Scofield in the Scofield Reference Bible, and continues to have wide influence through modern prophecy adherents such as Hal Lindsey, John Walvoord, Benny Hinn, John Hagee, and the "Left Behind" series of books.

This interpretation fails to recognize that the book was initially intended for a particular time (the late first century) and a particular people (the believers in Asia Minor) who faced a particular set of circumstances (persecution by the Romans, both real and perceived). It also fails to appreciate the unique characteristics of apocalyptic literature. ⛊

Understanding Revelation is less about decoding cryptic information and more about sharing John's experience of an almighty God who rules over all things and all times. For this reason, reading passages aloud and sensing the power of the imagery can sometimes be more helpful than trying to dissect inscrutable puzzles. ⛊

The purpose of books like Revelation is not so much to forecast what happens in the future as to assure believers that God is in control of the future.

A dramatic reading: Several scholars have noted that the book of Revelation has a number of similarities to Greek dramas that were popular at the time. James Blevins, for example, suggests that the 24 elders in Revelation could be compared to the chorus that was an integral part of Greek plays. He identifies a number of passages as hymns, and outlines the book as a progression of seven acts, each containing seven scenes.[2]

For Reflection: *What has been your understanding of Revelation in the past? Does the approach taken here—that the book is not a detailed forecast of future events but an encouragement to present Christians living through great trials—make the book more or less challenging to you?*

A MESSAGE FOR A PROPHET
(vv. 1-3)

John begins his testimony by putting readers (or hearers) on notice that what follows is no ordinary writing: it is a revelation (*apocalypsis*) depicted as being both from and about Jesus Christ. ♆

The purpose of the revelation, John says, is to show Christ's servants "what must soon take place." This may bring us pause when we stop to realize that the epoch-changing events John spoke about did not in fact take place "soon," unless one rationalizes that "soon" in God's time may seem like forever in our time.

John apparently believed that the persecution of Christians was increasing, evil was ramping up its influence, and the only solution would be for God to bring about cataclysmic, world-changing events. That nearly 2,000 years have passed without such events does not change the core message of the book: Christians are challenged, in whatever circumstances, to remain faithful to God. As Mitchell Reddish puts it, "The importance of John's message lies not in chronology, but in theology."[3]

John claims to have received his revelations from Christ or an angelic representative of Christ (1:12-18), and to have written a faithful testimony to the words he heard and "even to all that he saw" (v. 2). This is a reminder that John's revelations came in a series of visions, experiences that often stretch language to and beyond its limits.

♆ **Objective and subjective:** In the opening line, "Jesus Christ" is in the genitive case, and could be interpreted as an objective genitive (from Jesus Christ) or a subjective genitive (about Jesus Christ). It is also possible that both meanings are intended: the message comes through an angel sent by Jesus, but it is also largely about Jesus. The translation "of Jesus Christ" captures the ambiguity of the revelation being both from Jesus and about Jesus.

GRACE FOR THE CHURCHES
(vv. 4-6)

The first two verses serve as an extended title of the book, after which John offers a blessing for those who read aloud and hear its "words of the prophecy" and keep them (v. 3). Few people in John's time would have a personal copy of Revelation or any other book, but they could have heard it read aloud in church, appreciating the dramatic nature of its content. John's contemporaries would not have a copy of the book to parse and analyze in an attempt to construct a timetable for the second coming: they would simply be overwhelmed by the imagery and reminded that God is Lord of the present and the future, the living and the dead.

As mentioned above, the introduction and conclusion of the apocalypse have the form of a letter, and in v. 4 we find the address: John writes to "the seven churches that are in Asia," the western part of what used to be called Asia Minor (now Turkey), near the coast of the Aegean Sea. ⬇

To the churches, John extends grace from God, from "the seven spirits who are before his throne," and from Jesus Christ (v. 4). The reference to God as the one "who was and who is and who is to come" is repeated in 1:8 and 4:8.

Some readers think of the seven spirits as seven archangels who do God's bidding, but it is probably best to think of the seven spirits as a rough equivalent of the Holy Spirit, of God's divine presence at work in the world (compare the use of sevens and the "seven eyes of the LORD, which range through the whole world" in Zech. 4:2, 10, which has an apocalyptic flavor). Seven is an important number in religious thought for a variety of reasons, and is the most significant of several numbers that play important roles in Revelation, where 3, 10, 12, and 24 also figure prominently.

⬇ **The seven churches**: By the end of the first century, there were almost certainly more than seven churches in Asia Minor. Perhaps the seven addressed by John were considered to be the more prominent or influential ones. The churches addressed in chs. 2-3 were in the cities of Ephesus, Smyrna, Pergamum, Thyatira, Sardis, Philadelphia, and Laodicea.

Some imaginative interpreters have seen the seven churches as symbolic of the church in various ages, inevitably imagining the present age as the last, and particularly subject to the charges of being "lukewarm" that were levied against the church at Laodicea. This was almost certainly not John's intent: he was writing to specific churches at a specific time, speaking to specific situations with which he was familiar. Even so, the issues faced in those churches have a universal aspect, and may be applicable to modern churches as well.

John describes Christ as "the faithful witness," "the firstborn of the dead," "the ruler of the kings of the earth," the one "who loves us and freed us from our sins by his blood, and made us to be a kingdom, priests serving his God and Father" (vv. 5-6a).

This latter imagery is drawn from Exod. 19:6, in which God promised to make Israel a "kingdom of priests." Other Exodus themes will follow: the Roman emperor is like a new pharaoh who must be deposed through plagues, signs, and wonders so that God's people may pass safely through the sea. Only Christ, as ruler over all other kings, could accomplish this. ⏬

> ⏬ **The sea:** For the ancients, the sea was a symbol of chaos, something far too massive for humans to ever control. A common divine attribute is the ability to reign in the power of the sea, as God did in Exodus and as Jesus did in calming the stormy sea. One of the most powerful claims in the book of Revelation, then, is "the sea was no more" (Rev. 21:1b).

For Reflection: *Think about the world in which you live, both locally and globally. Are there metaphorical emperors or pharaohs that you would like to see overthrown before justice can reign and believers can rest secure?*

GOOD NEWS FOR BELIEVERS
(vv. 7-8)

Apocalyptic literature, as we have noted, grew from troubled times when believers perceived their position as being so dire and the world so evil that their only hope was for God to intervene in history and usher in a new age. John saw his era as such a time, when the best news he could offer was that Christ would soon be "coming with the clouds" so that "every eye will see him" (v. 7).

This mental picture, though immensely popular in hymnody and pulpit rhetoric, should be understood as a metaphor rather than a specific description of the manner of Christ's return.

The image of Jesus surfing through the heavens on a billowy cloud is appealing, but such theatrics would only be visible within a limited horizon. Like all people of his day, John envisioned a flat earth that would allow all people a common plane of vision to the highest reaches of the sky. The point of the metaphor is that when Christ returns, in some fashion everyone on earth will know it—friend and foe alike. ⏬

⊍ **Coming in the clouds:** This imagery is not new to John. While the stories of Israel's wilderness wandering often speak of Yahweh (the LORD) as appearing in a cloud, Isa. 19:1 speaks of Yahweh riding on a swift cloud to vanquish the Egyptians, and Ps. 68:4 describes God as "him who rides on the clouds." Matthew cites Jesus as predicting that he would return by "coming on the clouds" (Matt. 24:30, 26:64). As he often does, John picked up on metaphorical language from both Hebrew and Christian traditions.

John's double affirmation (literally "Yes! Amen!") is reinforced by one of the few statements directly attributed to God in the Apocalypse. God self-identifies, according to John, as "the Alpha and Omega ... who was and is and is to come, the Almighty."

Alpha and Omega are the first and last letters in the Greek alphabet. When John uses the same expression in 21:6 (attributed to God) and 22:13 (attributed to Christ), he adds "the first and the last." This expression, a literary device called a "merism," uses the beginning and the end to indicate everything in between, an artistic way of insisting that God's presence pervades all times and all places.

God's "Alpha and Omega" existence from beginning to end is further emphasized with the words "who was, and is, and is to come," which repeats a phrase from v. 4 that will be repeated again in 4:8. God is likewise "the Almighty." Believers can trust God as the creative prime mover of all things, the sustaining power behind the present world, and the one who can be trusted to bring all things to completion.

What does this curious text have to say for modern believers who don't live under persecution, but who do face daily difficulties and the constant temptation to assimilate fully to a culture that has no place for God?

When we face violence, poverty, terrorism, and other threats that seem to make the world a desperately forlorn place, we too can trust in a God whose rule is supreme, and who offers the hope of a brighter future where justice will prevail and the righteous will be vindicated.

For Reflection: *What obstacles to faithful and joyful living are foremost in your life? Does John's promise of Christ's return offer encouragement to you?*

THE HARDEST QUESTION
Is Revelation a dangerous book?

Should we really encourage people to study Revelation? Improper interpretations of the book could be not only unfortunate, but also dangerous, especially in the light of political and religious tensions in the Middle East.

The persons who seem most fascinated by the book of Revelation tend to be a group within fundamentalism known as premillennial dispensationalists. Adherents of this view, popularized by the Scofield Reference Bible and books such as Hal Lindsey's *Late Great Planet Earth*, believe that Revelation, interpreted along with Daniel 7-12, Ezekiel 38-39, and the little apocalypses of Mark 13, Matthew 24, and Luke 21, offers a timeline of literal events that will take place before a world-ending battle they believe will actually take place at "Armageddon," a reference to the ancient city of Megiddo (*har-megiddo* means "the mountain of Megiddo").

Megiddo, like Hazor to the north, was located on an impressive hill beside the Via Maris, the main highway that ran from Egypt and through Palestine before connecting with trade routes to Lebanon in the north and Mesopotamia to the east.

Because of its strategic position, Megiddo was a constant target for conquest. As a result, archaeologists have uncovered as many as two dozen layers of civilization, as city after city was conquered and burned before a new city was built on top of the old. Megiddo's history of warfare made it a natural symbol as a place of future conflict.

A gold-plated menorah constructed by the Temple Institute, said to be for the Third Temple

For many years, both dispensationalists and some ultra-orthodox Jews have promoted the building of a third temple in Jerusalem, hoping to replace the one destroyed by the Romans in 70 CE. While some ultra-orthodox avoid Temple Mount for fear of stepping on the former location of the Holy of Holies, others want to build a new temple and re-establish the practice of animal sacrifice. An ultra-orthodox organization known as the Temple Institute has become particularly popular among American dispensationalists, attracting them to a "museum" where adherents have on display furnishings, equipment, and even an altar they are making in hopes of using them in a third temple. These include a huge gold-plated menorah that is currently mounted on a hill in full view of the Temple Mount.

Why is this a problem? The Temple Mount, by longstanding agreement, is under the control of Muslim religious authorities. For the past 1300 years, the area has been occupied by the Al Aqsa Mosque and the Dome of the Rock, sacred buildings that go back to the seventh century CE. Jerusalem's Temple Mount is the third holiest site in Islam.

No new temple could be built there unless the mosques were destroyed and the Muslims were evicted—which would almost certainly incite a war that could be far more widespread than Armaggedon and make World War II look like a regional conflict.

What relation could a misreading of the book of Revelation have to this? Some dispensationalists not only believe that the events depicted in Daniel and Revelation will be literally fulfilled, but also that they require the presence of an earthly temple (sometimes known as "Ezekiel's temple") so that a coming "antichrist" can defile it in accordance with their understanding of end-times prophecy. As a result, dispensationalists have provided substantial financial and moral support for groups such as the Temple Institute, hoping that they can play a role in fulfilling their view of prophecy and speeding up the end times.

This interpretation of Daniel and Revelation, as anyone who pays attention to world events can see, feeds into the hopes of people whose actions could lead to catastrophic results for the rest of the world.

When read in a popular and literalist way, the book of Revelation has the potential to be a very dangerous book indeed. That is one reason why it is important for thinking Christians to study the book and develop a more appropriate understanding of what John's Apocalypse does—and does not—intend to teach us.

NOTES

[1]Mitchell G. Reddish, *Revelation,* Smyth & Helwys Commentary (Macon, GA: Smyth & Helwys, 2001), 29.

[2]James Blevins, "Revelation, Book of" in the *Mercer Dictionary of the Bible* (Macon, GA: Mercer University Press, 1990), 759-61.

[3]Reddish, *Revelation,* 33.

Revelation 5:1-14

SONGS OF ANGELS

Worthy is the Lamb that was slaughtered
to receive power and wealth and wisdom and might
and honor and glory and blessing!
—Revelation 5:12

God's in his heaven—all's right with the world! That famous line, from Robert Browning's "Pippa Passes" (1841), is stark in its innocence compared to some of the sordid scenes in the lengthy poetic play. But is it true? If God's in heaven, is all right with the world? The book of Revelation has a lot to say about God's heavenly throne room, but John's comforting vision was given to people who knew very well that all was *not* right with the world.

Writing in the late first century, when Christians were a scorned minority and sporadic outbreaks of persecution could make life fearful and despairing, John's apocalyptic visions declared that despite the world's wrongness, God remained on the throne and would one day make things right.

With few exceptions, Christians in today's world do not live under oppression, but even so we perceive a world gone wrong. Global warming, international conflicts, tribal warfare, religion-inspired terrorism, economic disasters, senseless gun violence, domestic abuse, and countless personal crises can make for a gloomy outlook.

If all is not right with the world, is there still hope?

John thought so.

A SCROLL
(vv. 1-5)

After proclaiming Christ's message to the seven churches of Asia (chs. 2-3), providing useful texts for a multitude of ready-made sermon series, John turns to an elaborate description of the heavenly throne room, stretching language to the breaking point in his attempt to portray its glittering grandeur.

In his vision, God's throne was guarded by four exotic creatures and surrounded by 24 elders on lesser thrones, with all in the room engaged in constant worship of God as the creator of all things (4:11). The "four living creatures" around the throne, one each in the general shape of a lion, an ox, an eagle, and a man, were said to have six wings each, and to be "full of eyes all around and inside" (4:6-8). The bizarre imagery, like many other word pictures in the book, is intended to be metaphorical rather than literal. How could John know that the creatures had eyes on the inside? And why would they? ⛊

John seemed most impressed that the creatures were living—as opposed to the winged animal figures or cherubim of stone that typically flanked the thrones of earthly kings. The three pairs of wings give the impression that the creatures were highly mobile, able to fly in any direction at a moment's notice. The eyes both inside (4:6-8) and out suggest that they were intensely perceptive; that nothing escaped their attention.

⛊**Strange creatures:** The image of the four cherubim has much in common with Ezekiel's vision of four winged human/animal cherubim who surrounded and moved God's heavenly chariot (Ezek. 1:4-14, 10:1-22). Winged cherubim covered in gold stood atop the Ark of the Covenant (Exod. 25:19, 37:8), and even larger ones were constructed to overshadow the ark in the "Holy of Holies" in Solomon's temple (1 Kgs. 6:23-28).

An early church tradition drew symbolic representations for the four Gospel writers from this scene: Matthew was imagined as the man-like figure, Mark as the lion, Luke as the ox, and John as the eagle. There is nothing in the scriptures to substantiate this connection.

This colossal lamassu, more than 16 feet tall and weighing 40 tons, was one of two cherub-like figures that once flanked the entrance to the throne room of the Assyrian king Sargon II at his palace in Dur-Sharru-kin (modern Khorsabad). Thought of as a protective spirit, the figure has six horns curled around its head, symbolic of deity. Sargon, whose name (*sharru-kin*) means "true king," began construction of the palace a few years after the Assyrians had conquered Israel in 722 BCE.

While these characteristics would lead the reader to think of them primarily as guards who protected the throne and stood ready to do God's bidding, their main function in John's vision was to lead the worship of God. As they sang "Holy, holy, holy, the Lord God Almighty, who was and is and is to come," the 24 elders would also fall to the ground, casting their crowns before the throne and adding their own chorus of praise to God as creator. ⚓

In ch. 5 the scene remains the same, but the focus shifts from the praise of God as the worthy creator to the need for someone worthy enough to break the seven seals of a mysterious scroll containing an itinerary of things yet to come.

No one "in heaven or on earth or under the earth" proved able to open the scroll, leading John to weep bitterly that its contents would remain a mystery (v. 4). John's despair builds dramatic tension, but soon one of the elders told him to stanch his tears, for "the Lion of the tribe of Judah, the Root of David, has conquered so that he can open the seven seals" (v. 5). ⚓

Both images are drawn from concepts found in the Hebrew Bible. Jacob's blessing to his son Judah in Gen. 49:9-10 described Judah as a "lion's whelp" to whom the kingship would belong: "the scepter shall not depart from Judah." David was descended from the tribe of Judah, and God promised him that his descendants would always sit upon the throne (2 Samuel 7). After the Babylonians conquered Judah and destroyed Jerusalem in 587 BCE, the Hebrews held to the hope that God would raise up a scion of David to rule again, speaking of

---

⚓ **The 24 elders**: Exactly what the 24 elders are meant to represent is uncertain. One early church tradition that remains popular is that they signified the 12 tribes of Israel and the 12 apostles, thus representing the totality of God's people through both Israel and the church.

The elders' dress and golden crowns suggest a kingly role, combined with the priestly role of worship as they offered incense and prayers to God.

⚓ **The lion of Judah**: Some Jewish writers, as evidenced by the Apocrypha, saw the reference to the "lion of Judah" as an indication that the coming messiah would be a fierce military man who would lead Israel to victory through violence.

The Testament of Judah clearly identified the "lion of Judah" from Gen. 49:9-10 with the coming messiah (24:5), and 2 Esdras 12:31-32—written at about the same time as Revelation—declared "the lion is . . . the messiah."[1]

⛏ **An unusual scroll**: The scroll John describes is unusual for several reasons. We should point out, first, that the Greek word *biblion* has the basic meaning of "book," as in a lengthy writing. It usually refers to books of multiple pages, but could also describe a book in scroll form. Scrolls were still more common in John's day, though codexes made of separate pages bound together largely replaced them early in the second century.

John is almost certainly referring to a rolled-up scroll, since it could be "sealed with seven seals" much more easily than a codex. The seals were blobs of melted wax into which the author's personal seal or an official's seal of office had been pressed. Most letters or documents bore a single seal, and only the intended recipient had the authority to break the seal and open it.

The multiple seals—with seven being a number that indicates perfection or completeness—emphasize the importance and serious nature of the scroll, which is also unusual in that it has writing on both the front and the back. Scrolls were usually written on one side only, though a short description or summary of its contents might be written on the outermost part.

The writing on both sides may be an indication that the message is so long that a single scroll could not contain it on one side. Or, since the scroll was fully written on both sides, there was no room for anything else to be added, so it could be considered "the last word."

him as the "root" or "branch" of David, or from the stump of Jesse, David's father (see Isa. 11:1, 10; Jer. 23:5, 33:15; Zech. 3:8, 6:12). ⛏

The "lion who has conquered," of course, is a reference to Jesus—but when John looked for the approach of a powerful carnivore who wins victories by strength and violence, he was overcome with amazement: the lion was a lamb.

For Reflection: *How do you respond to the strange imagery of John's visions? Do you find them appealing, or just plain bizarre? If God sent a vision to encourage you today, do you think the images would be different? What kinds of images might communicate better to you?*

A LAMB
(vv. 6-10)

Without comment on the shocking switch between what he heard and what he saw, John describes the appearance of a lamb standing in the midst of the heavenly council, but it was no ordinary lamb. It stood "as if it had been slaughtered"—bearing the marks of slaughter, but clearly alive and still standing.

The reader has no doubt that the lamb represents Jesus Christ, who had stood amid his disciples with the marks of execution still painfully evident. The image of a lamb becomes the most common title or description of Christ in the book, occurring some 29 times. 🔯

For a lamb, the mark of slaughter would be a slit throat, but John does not dwell on specifics, and we have no more need to try visualizing that gory image than we do trying to fit seven horns and seven eyes on the lamb's head.

Once again, John uses metaphorical language. A lamb with seven horns and seven eyes would be beyond freakish, though people have tried to portray it graphically, as a quick Google search can show.

We gain nothing by dwelling on how the curious collection of eyes and horns might appear: the purpose of John's imagery was to signify the power and pervasiveness of Christ. From ancient times, horns have been symbolic of power. In the Babylonian traditions especially, powerful gods and earthly kings were routinely portrayed with several sets of horns wrapped around their heads.

🔯 **Christ as a lamb**: The most common title for Christ in the book of Revelation is that of a lamb. It appears 29 times, each time using the word *arnion*. The New Testament uses lamb terminology in reference to Christ just four other times (John 1:29, 36; Acts 8:32; 1 Pet. 1:19), but each of those uses the term *amnos*.

Arnion is a diminutive form of the word that can refer to sheep of any age, but it is usually translated as "lamb" because of the sacrificial imagery associated with it. But, as David Aune points out, little lambs don't have horns, only male rams. So, it would be equally possible to translate the word as "ram" in reference to Christ.[2]

The distinction can't be stretched too far: while rams do have horns, they don't typically have seven of them.

The appearance of the lamb resolves the dramatic problem that no one had been found who was able to break the seven seals and reveal the scroll's secretive contents. The lamb's worthiness is seen in the marks of its willing sacrifice and the strength symbolized by the seven horns. The number seven indicated completeness, showing that Christ had full power to accomplish the task.

The eyes, John says, are "the seven spirits of God sent out into all the earth." As with the "seven spirits" before the throne in 1:4, the image appears

♱ **A new song:** The singing of a new song appears in the Psalms as a special way of giving praise to God, often in the context of victory. Psalm 98, for example, begins with a call to worship: "O sing to the LORD a new song, for he has done marvelous things. His right hand and his mighty arm have gotten him victory" (Ps. 98:1).

Similar references to a "new song" are found in Ps. 33:3, 40:3, 96:1, 144:9, and Isa. 42:10.

As Mitchell Reddish notes, the song is not only "new" in being heard for the first time, but new in the sense that it is qualitatively different: "It celebrates God's decisive act of salvation enacted through the sacrificial death of Jesus" whose sacrificial death has "ransomed" believers from every nation and station of life, making them "a kingdom and priests serving our God."[3]

equivalent to the Holy Spirit, and we may understand the lamb's "eyes" in the same way. The vision declared that the lamb standing ready to unseal the scroll was worthy enough, powerful enough, and perceptive enough to accomplish the task, as evidenced by the "new song" of the living creatures and the elders in vv. 9-10. ♱

The most surprising aspect to readers is that the lamb's worthiness and victory did not come through brute force, but through self-sacrifice. The hymn of praise says nothing about the lamb's powerful horns or all-seeing eyes, but centers on Christ's willingness to die for the sake of the people "from every tribe and language and people and nation." This is the source of his power and the secret to his victory.

For Reflection: *How does this image of the lamb compare with the Gospels' portrayal of Jesus' death and resurrection?*

A CHORUS
(vv. 11-14)

The voices of the living creatures and the 24 elders were soon amplified by innumerable angels ("myriads of myriads and thousands of thousands") who joined the chorus.

The Greek word *myriades*, from which our word "myriad" derives, was sometimes used to mean 10,000, but more commonly referred to a countless number. The doubly emphatic "myriads of myriads and thousands of thousands" is clearly designed to describe a multitude beyond counting.

Try to imagine the bone-chilling sound of such a heavenly chorus in full voice singing "Worthy is the lamb that was slaughtered to receive power and wealth and wisdom and might and glory and honor and blessing!" (v. 11b).

As if the hosts of heaven could not proffer sufficient praise, to their voices were added every creature in heaven, on the earth, under the earth, and in the sea. Not only all people, but also every creature in the universe joined to sing an eternal blessing "to the one seated on the throne, and to the Lamb" (v. 13). ♛

While the song addressed both "the one seated on the throne" and the lamb who stood before it, the emphasis is on the lamb, who is declared worthy because of his atoning death. As the song reaches its crescendo, the scene arrives at its climax as the four living creatures cried "Amen" and the elders prostrated themselves in worship before God, the author of all creation, and the lamb, who had been found worthy to open the scroll (v. 14). ♛

We should not forget the context. The heavenly praise engenders enthralling thoughts, but remains an accompaniment to the dramatic action in which the lamb has been revealed as the only one worthy to break the seven seals of the scroll.

The entire chapter, then, serves as an introduction to what will follow the opening of the scroll, a series of catastrophic judgments and descriptions of suffering that will encompass chs. 6-19, the largest part of the book. The lamb's

♛**Universal praise**: The "new song" of praise to Christ is reflected in a number of Christian hymns, including the familiar "Worthy Is the Lamb" and "All Hail the Power of Jesus' Name."

John's concept of the universe, like others of his day, consisted of a flat but circular earth containing both land and sea, covered by a huge domelike "firmament" above which were the heavens. Sheol, the world of the dead (both righteous and unrighteous) was thought to be beneath the surface of the earth.

Thus, John's reference to all creatures in heaven, on the earth, under the earth, and in the sea was a way of saying "every creature in the universe."

♛ **Three in one**: The song of praise to "the one seated on the throne" (God) "and to the Lamb" (Jesus) whose seven eyes are the "seven spirits of God" (the Holy Spirit) indicates how closely John held these three aspects of God's personhood, distinct in some ways but inseparable in others.

The early church would not officially work out and adopt the doctrine of the Trinity until the Council of Nicea in 325, but texts such as this one show that its roots are present in scripture.

ability to break the seals does not simply allow the scroll to be opened and read, but sets in motion the events it describes.

With its alien setting and strange characters, we might wonder what profit there is in studying a text like this. How might it speak to our needs in our time?

To answer that, we return to our opening thoughts. All is *not* right with the world—not with our world any more than John's world. Yet, we can hold the belief that God is on the throne, that all is not lost.

While the imagery of the creator God's rule over the universe is powerful and encouraging, John's vision also exalts Christ as one who triumphed through suffering, ensuring eternal security for the believer.

The lamb's wounds, still evident from slaughter, are a reminder that suffering is ongoing. Eternal security does not equate to present protection. We face many obstacles in this life, some of our own making, some beyond our control. Trouble comes, even to the righteous. The world can be dark and hard and evil, and sometimes it seems to be spiraling into oblivion.

Yet, in the midst of our trials, John insists, God is on the throne. Christ has won the victory. Like people in bondage who dare to raise hope to the heavens, we can sing a new song of praise to the one who was, who is, and who is to come, trusting that God holds both the universe and our future in faithful and worthy hands.

For Reflection: *What's wrong with your world? As alien as they may seem to us, do John's visions offer you the hope of better days?*

THE HARDEST QUESTION
Where does providence come in?

The approach we've taken in this lesson acknowledges that the world can be a hard place where good people suffer, but also affirms a belief that God rules the universe and will one day make all things right. Really?

The term for this belief is "providence," but people holding to different theological traditions interpret that term in different ways. Those who take a more Calvinistic approach contend that God not only holds the future, but also actively controls what happens on earth. When this belief is amplified by fundamentalism, everything from killer hurricanes to mass murders are imagined as divine judgments on America's collective sin, or as inscrutable acts that have some divine purpose we cannot yet determine.

Thus, many people commonly declare a belief that "everything happens for a reason," a fatalistic approach that absolves them of personal responsibility by putting everything on God, and avoids the sharp question of "Why?" by assigning both success and sorrow to divine engagement in human life.

This deterministic view is neither satisfactory nor supported by the whole of scripture. Such a view, Reddish notes, "robs human life of any real meaning or significance, for then human thoughts and actions are merely acted-out roles in a cosmic script."[4]

A better understanding of providence, and the one taken in the book of Revelation, recognizes human freedom to do good or evil, with consequences that affect not only themselves, but others. Believing in God's providence does not necessitate believing that God constantly interferes in daily life, orchestrating what happens for purposes known only in heaven.

The world is what it is: a place where people can be greedy and hateful and violent—or generous and loving and kind. Sometimes, there is no apparent connection between our behavior and our circumstances: wicked people may prosper and the righteous may suffer. God cannot be expected to step into every situation with immediate rewards or retributions: if that were the case, only complete fools would continue to walk a wicked path with punishment awaiting at every turn.

The seeming absence of God from directing events in this present world, however, does not preclude a belief that God reigns and will one day set things right. God is the Alpha and the Omega, John insists, the beginning and the end. If God was capable of creating all things, then God is surely capable of bringing history to an appropriate conclusion.

It is such a belief that infused John's Apocalypse with hope that though the world can be a dark and deadly place soaked with suffering, a day is coming when God will make all things right.

NOTES

[1] For more on the popularity of lion imagery and the important relationship between the lion and the lamb, see Eugene Boring, *Revelation*, Interpretation: A Bible Commentary for Teaching and Preaching (Louisville, KY: John Knox Press, 1989), 108-111.

[2] David Aune, *Revelation 1-6*, Word Biblical Commentary, Vol. 52a (Nashville: Word Books, 1997), 323.

[3] Mitchell G. Reddish, *Revelation*, Smyth & Helwys Bible Commentary (Macon, GA: Smyth & Helwys, 2001), 111.

[4] Ibid., 116.

Revelation 7:1-17

TRANSFORMING TERROR

They cried out in a loud voice, saying,
"Salvation belongs to our God who is seated on the throne, and to the Lamb!
—Revelation 7:10

We use the word "terrorism" a lot these days, and news reports of various atrocities give us a constant second- or third-hand taste of it. Revelation 7:1-17 comes as an interlude in a section of Revelation so terror-laden that John's hearers and modern readers need a break from the horror just to find hope enough to continue.

Earlier (5:1-14), John described a vision focused on a special scroll bearing seven seals, and the search for someone who was worthy to break the seals and reveal its contents. Christ was introduced, first as a lion, then as a slaughtered-but-living lamb, as the only one qualified for the task. The section closed with uncountable angels praising God the creator and Christ the redeemer.

That happy note came to an end with the breaking of the first seal and the awareness that the opening of the scroll would unleash terrible judgments upon the earth, ranging from famine to pestilence to war and cosmic catastrophes.

With the opening of the first seal, John heard one of the four living creatures around the throne cry "Come!" and a white horse rode forth bearing a crowned rider who had power to conquer all who stood before him (6:1-2).

The second seal led to a second cry and the loosing of a bright red horse whose rider was given a great sword and the ability to take peace from the earth, so that "people would slaughter one other" (6:3-4).

A third seal and cry brought a black horse whose rider carried a set of scales used to show how exorbitantly expensive food would become during a time of great famine (6:5-6).

The fourth seal and a cry from the fourth living creature loosed a pale green horse, the color of a deathly pallor, whose rider would bring death through sword, pestilence, famine, and even wild animals of the earth (6:7-8).

The four initial judgments were followed by the breaking of the fifth seal, which revealed a vision of martyrs crying for vengeance from beneath the heavenly altar, but being told to wait a little longer, until the number of those to be killed for their faith would be complete (6:9-11).

As if the first five seals were not bad enough, the sixth one unleashed a series of cosmic cataclysms: earthquakes and atmospheric events (due to volcanic eruptions?) that blackened the sun and made the moon appear red as "stars fell to the earth" like ripe figs falling in a windstorm. Mountains moved and the sky disappeared, leaving people of every station, from kings to slaves, begging the mountains to hide them "from the face of the one seated on the throne and from the wrath of the lamb" (6:12-17).

Careful readers who absorb such horrors may find themselves emotionally exhausted, hardly able to bear any more. The interlude, then, is welcome.

A VISION ON EARTH
(vv. 1-8)

Between the sixth and seventh seals, John relates two parenthetical accounts, each introduced by "After this I saw . . .," which is John's way of indicating separate visions (see also 4:1, 7:1, 15:5, 18:1). The first vision is set on earth (7:1-8), and the second in heaven (7:9-17).

The earthly vision declares that God will halt the horrors, here symbolized by destructive winds, and send an angel bearing a seal with which to mark 144,000 persons: 12,000 each from the 12 tribes of Israel. ◗

This text is used by Jehovah's Witnesses to contend that only 144,000 people will attain heaven, and employed by dispensationalists to argue that 144,000 Jews will be marked for a special evangelistic purpose during the last days. ◗ Both positions require a literalist manipulation of the texts that is not supported by an understanding of the apocalyptic (and hence highly metaphorical) nature of the John's writing.

John's word pictures were probably designed to indicate a large but not necessarily specific number of believers who would be "sealed" during the time of tribulation, which he believed had already begun. The reference to the 12 tribes of Israel could indicate an understanding of the church as the "New Israel," and does not necessarily refer to Jewish persons only (cf. Jas. 1:1).

The protection of the seal did not remove the 144,000 from suffering, as some contend, but marked them as belonging to Christ. It is likely that the number refers to the martyrs who had died for Christ, a number that was still incomplete in 6:11. As a multiple of both 10 and 12, the 144,000 may have symbolized the complete (but not literal) number of those who would die in the time of trial.

> **For Reflection:** *How have you heard the 144,000 described before? Do you think it points to a literal accounting of people? What do you think is the most likely significance of the number?*

⛉ Twelve tribes: The Bible lists the tribes of Israel in about 20 places, and the lists do not always contain the same tribes or even the same number of tribes. In Genesis 49, Jacob blessed his 12 sons, who became the eponymous ancestors of the tribes.

In many later lists, the tribe of Joseph was split into two tribes named after his sons Ephraim and Manasseh, and these became the dominant tribes in the north (sometimes they are referred to as "half-tribes"). With the splitting of Joseph into two, the tribe of Levi, which was scattered in levitical cities throughout the other tribal lands, dropped from the list, maintaining the number 12 (as in the list at Num. 1:20-43).

A list in Deuteronomy 33 maintains both Joseph and Levi as tribes, but does not mention the tribe of Simeon, which was surrounded by and largely assimilated into Judah. While this list has only 11 tribes, another list in Judges 5 includes just 10. That list does not include Simeon, Levi, Joseph, Manasseh, or even Judah, but adds tribes named Machir and Gilead.

John's list in Rev. 7:5-8 includes both Joseph and Manasseh as well as Levi, but not Ephraim, and it eliminates Dan to keep the number at 12. The tribe of Dan had been allotted land in the heart of Palestine, but was unable to claim it from its Canaanite inhabitants (Josh. 19:47ff; Judges 18), so the tribe migrated northward and took the city of Laish (or Leshem) as a home, renaming it Dan and becoming the northernmost tribe. The tribe of Dan was also famous for the worship of an idol, however (Judg. 18:14-20), and as the home of an Israelite temple containing a golden calf (1 Kgs. 12:25-30), so it fell from favor in some circles.

While most tribal lists begin with Reuben, Jacob's oldest son, John's enumeration in Revelation begins with Judah, the tribe from which Jesus descended.

⇓ **A dispensationalist view:** An interpretation of the end times called "dispensationalism" was developed in the 19th century by J. N. Darby, then further refined and popularized by C. I. Scofield in the pervasive "Scofield Reference Bible," which promoted the view in footnotes that some readers considered nearly as inspired as the King James text. It gained additional popularity through fundamentalist TV evangelists and books such as Hal Lindsay's *The Late Great Planet Earth*, and some facets of it continue to be spread through books such as the popular "Left Behind" series by Tim LaHaye and Jerry Jenkins.

Dispensationalism holds that human history can be divided into seven dispensations, or epochs, in which God deals in successively different ways with humans, who inevitably fail to meet God's expectations. The church age or "age of grace" is seen as the sixth dispensation, with the coming "millennium," believed to be a literal thousand-year period, to be the seventh.

The most popular dispensationalist view is called pre-millennial dispensationalism. According to this viewpoint, God has different destinies in mind for Israel and the church, which are seen as separate entities. Most who hold this position also maintain a "pre-tribulational" view of Christ's return, believing that he will first come to "rapture" believers into heaven, with those who remain facing a seven-year "great tribulation," during which 144,000 Jews will follow Christ. Afterward, they believe, Christ will return again, accompanied by the saints, to rule on earth for 1,000 years. The millennium would then be followed by the last judgment and the creation of a new heaven and new earth.

This belief is based primarily on a literal reading of selected texts from Daniel and Revelation. When one recognizes the pictorial language and symbolism common to apocalyptic works, the attempt to draw timetables that map out the future loses much of its appeal, as well as its validity.

A VISION IN HEAVEN
(vv. 9-12)

The second parenthetical vision shifts John's focus from earthly tribulation to heavenly splendor. John is shown the heavenly court where God sits on a great throne, accompanied by Christ as a lamb with seven eyes that represent the pervasive Spirit of God. The throne is guarded and served by four supernatural "living creatures" and surrounded by 24 crowned elders on lesser thrones. These were joined by countless angels who united in singing praise to God and to the lamb.

Now, John sees before the throne "a great multitude that no one could count." John emphasizes the crowd's inclusive nature: the people come "from every nation, from all tribes and peoples and languages" (v. 9a). This recalls God's promise to Abraham that all nations of the earth would be blessed through him and his descendants (Gen. 12:1-3; see also Isa. 49:6).

Some interpreters think of the multitude as an image of the entire church through the ages, but John probably saw them as an uncountable host of martyrs. They wear white robes and bear palm branches as symbols of victory, but "they have 'won' only from the heavenly perspective of the Lamb's definition of winning; on earth they have been killed."[1]

Although the multitude of martyrs gave their lives for Christ, even that did not earn them salvation, for salvation is God's alone. The multitude testified: "Salvation belongs to our God who is seated on the throne, and to the Lamb!"

As in ch. 5, where the song of the living creatures and the elders was joined by a host of angels, the cry of the martyrs swelled with the addition of all the inhabitants of heaven singing a seven-fold blessing to God.

The human celebrants seemed to be singing a responsive hymn in conjunction with the heavenly beings who devote themselves to serving and praising God. Their function is described in v. 15 with the Greek word *latreuō*, which means both "worship" and "serve."

In biblical thought, and particularly in John's apocalypse, seven is an especially significant number, and the heavenly hosts celebrated seven specific attributes that belong to God: blessing, glory, wisdom, thanksgiving, honor, power, and might. The same list is found in 5:12, and serves as a sort of doxology.

Well and good, the reader may think, but what does it have to do with me? Let's consider two things. First, John's glimpse of glory leads us to imagine what it might be like to dwell eternally in the presence of God. It is an image of security and perfect harmony with God and all who stand before the throne.

Secondly, the picture may also suggest how God would have believers to live while on this earth—how the church of the present ought to look. We are familiar with a multitude of churches that cater to different preferences with regard to denomination, theology, worship style, or culture. In our world, that may be the best we can do, but the text suggests a day will come when all that separates us is overcome by the common desire to glorify the God who created all things and who saved us all in Christ Jesus. We don't have to wait until we get to heaven to hold forth the ideal of Christian unity that transcends ethnic, cultural, and theological boundaries. ⚜

For Reflection: *The people in this text are marked by the white robes they wear and the palm branches they bear. Is there anything that sets us apart from those who do not claim the name of Christ?*

⛏ **A living example:** Perhaps you have heard of Dr. Albert Schweitzer, who is remembered as a missionary, a physician, a musician, and a historical theologian. In a time when few people ever considered such a thing—and when he could have lived a very prosperous life in Europe—Schweitzer chose to give his life in serving the needs of those who lived in the African jungle. He was to the first half of the 20th century what Mother Teresa was to the second half. His life was a shining light, a brilliant example of what we are called to be.

Schweitzer observed that it was easy to be pessimistic when he looked at the world and its cruelty and pain and needs, but he was optimistic in his hopes for the world. He knew that such optimistic hopes depended on people giving of themselves to make the world a better place.

In a book titled *Out of My Life and Thought*, he said: "I could not but feel with a sympathy full of regret all the pain that I saw around me, not only that of men but that of the whole creation. From this community of suffering I have never tried to withdraw myself. It seemed to me a matter of course that we should all take our share of the burden of pain which lies upon the world."[2]

Schweitzer, like those people in Revelation robed in white, challenges us to ask ourselves if we are willing to take on our share of that burden of pain in the hope of bringing health to this world, and bringing more persons into the next world.

A QUESTION AND A HYMN
(vv. 13-17)

After observing this beautiful scene of the multitude singing together God's praise, the account moves to a question, as one of the elders asked John to identify the white-robed multitude. Like Ezekiel before him (Ezek. 37:3), John responded by confessing his ignorance: "Sir, you are the one that knows." ⛏

The elder offered a seemingly paradoxical statement: they were persons who have come through time of struggle, having "washed their robes and made them white in the blood of the Lamb" (v. 14).

⛏ **Teaching methods:** In ancient Hellenistic pedagogy, teachers often asked questions that their students could not hope to answer as a way of arousing curiosity and then sharing important information.

In apocalyptic works, a heavenly being often acted as a guide or interpreter for the person to whom the vision was revealed.

Aspects of both methods are reflected in Rev. 17:13-14, where one of the elders poses a question that John cannot answer.

Anyone who has tried to wash bloodstains from a white shirt knows that blood is not a bleach: it does not turn things white. ✏ Again, John is speaking metaphorically. The people have trusted in Christ, whose atoning death—through the shedding of his blood—effectively cleansed the stains of their human failings and set them right with God, no longer tarnished or torn or twisted by the world.

In modern churches, persons being baptized often wear white robes. In the early church, baptism was often a major, solemn ceremony. In some traditions, candidates engaged in a long period of preparation prior to baptism, usually on Easter. In ceremonies separated by gender, they would remove their old clothes and step naked before God into the baptismal waters. When they emerged from the water, they were given a new white robe to wear as a symbol of their new life.

✏ **Way too literal:** On the effectiveness of the "blood" as a cleanser, I once heard an elderly Sunday School teacher who held racist views insist that there would be no black people in heaven, because "they'll be washed in the blood, and they'll be white."

This is one of many examples of combining biblical literalism with the human desire to find scriptural support for a preconceived opinion.

In John's vision, the people dressed in white were those who had trusted Christ for forgiveness, and who had remained faithful through the trials and tribulations and temptations of this world, even though it cost them their lives.

The elder went on to describe the life of those who worship and serve before the throne of God. They will be secure in God's protection and free from hunger, thirst, and the desert sun, he said.

In another paradox, the lamb will become the shepherd, guiding those he has redeemed "to springs of the water of life, and God will wipe away every tear from their eyes." (v. 17). ✏

✏ **Two similar promises:** Revelation 7 says of the inhabitants of heaven: "They will hunger no more, and thirst no more; the sun will not strike them, nor any scorching heat; for the Lamb at the center of the throne will be their shepherd, and he will guide them to springs of the water of life, and God will wipe away every tear from their eyes" (vv. 16-17).

Many years before, in speaking of those who had endured the tribulation of exile in Babylon, Isaiah declared: ". . . they shall not hunger or thirst, neither scorching wind nor sun shall strike them down, for he who has pity on them will lead them, and by springs of water will guide them" (Isa. 49:10).

The last three verses of the text appear as three three-line stanzas. They sound more like the Hebrew prophets than the later apocalyptics, and bear a striking resemblance to the promises of Isa. 49:10.

John's vision offers the assurance of a time and a realm where God is at home with his people, dwelling with them, caring for all their physical, emotional, and spiritual needs. Those who are gathered around God's throne will "hunger no more, and thirst no more" (v. 16). In other words, we will be delivered from physical needs.

The vision also insists that God will supply all our spiritual needs. The Lamb of God will lead believers to "springs of the water of life" as sustenance for the soul.

Finally, the text asserts that God will fulfill all our emotional needs. God will "wipe away every tear." We may experience the catharsis of emotionally honest and cleansing tears, but they won't follow us through eternity, for God's own hand will dry them: we will know eternal cleansing.

This picture holds not only the hope that lies before us, but a challenge to the life that lies around us. When the church rises up to offer shelter, proclaim good news, and wipe away tears, we might just catch a glimpse of heaven on earth.

For Reflection: *How many hymns or popular songs can you name that focus on the blood of the Jesus? You may recall older hymns such as "There Is Power in the Blood," "There Is a Fountain Filled with Blood," "Nothing but the Blood," "The Blood Will Never Lose its Power," and "Are You Washed in the Blood?" Do you think the image still resonates? Can you name any contemporary songs that focus on the shed blood of Jesus?*

THE HARDEST QUESTION
What about the violent imagery in Revelation?

Although this text does not deal directly with the violence and vengeance common to much of Revelation, and which both precedes and follows it, we cannot appreciate John's vision of heaven without also giving heed to the visions of terror down below.

When the lamb opens the scroll in Rev. 6:1-8, the earth's inhabitants are stricken with horrors ranging from war to famine to pestilence and death. Christian martyrs cry out for vengeance (6:9-11), and such devastating events follow that the earthly population's greatest fear is facing "the wrath of the lamb" (6:12-17).

In later chapters we find hail mixed with blood and fire (8:7), along with seas and rivers of blood (8:8-11, 16:3-4). Horses are said to wade for 200 miles in blood that reaches their bridles: and that's just part of the ruination visited on the earth and its people.

How can we reconcile images of a loving savior with such horrifying scenes? How can we comprehend the notion that Christ who willingly suffered and who taught his followers to turn the other cheek could also stand for sinners facing eternal torment in his presence (14:10)?

Eugene Boring suggests four perspectives that may help us to understand the presence of the Apocalypse's violent and vindictive language.[3]

1. The givenness of John's situation of suffering

Apocalyptic writings, John's included, grew from periods of present suffering in which believers saw no hope other than a divine intervention. As evidenced by the imprecatory psalms (Pss. 35, 55, 69, 109, and 137), people who are pushed to the edge may express feelings of outrage and calls for revenge, even in the context of worship. Such cries are not necessarily personal, Boring notes, "but a plea for the justice of God to be made manifest publicly.[4]

2. John's appropriation of tradition

John's visions show similarity to other thought from the ancient Near East, including that of a mythical battle between a chaos monster who lived in the sea, constantly sought to unmake creation, and was overcome violently.

John would also have been familiar with Jewish apocalyptic writings in which it was a standard pattern for extreme violence to occur in the last days. The image of horses wading bridle-deep in blood, for example, was known from other writings (1 Enoch 100:3, 2 Esdras 15:35-36).

Divinely wrought disasters were familiar parts of the Hebrew Bible, with which John would have been familiar. The disasters wrought in Revelation 6-19, except for their scale, are not unlike the plagues sent against Egypt in Exodus 7-12.

Likewise, the notion of God's wrath (6:16-17, 11:18, 14:10, 16:19, 19:15) has deep roots in Israel's theology, and even that of the early church. Israel provoked God to wrath in the wilderness (Exod. 22:21-24, Deut. 9:7-8), and the prophets declared that Israel's sin would arouse divine retribution (Isa. 1:24, 9:19, 13:9; Jer. 4:4, 10:10; Ezek. 7:8, 13:13; Hos. 5:10, 13:11; Micah 5:15, among many others). Jesus spoke of the coming wrath (Matt. 3:7, John 3:36), as did Paul (Rom. 1:18, 2:5; 1 Thess. 1:10, 2:16, 5:19).

In some cases, imagery such as earthquakes, hail, and other cosmic events are "not punishment language, but theophany language: the earth reels because it cannot stand in the presence of God."[5]

3. John's use of language

Boring notes that none of the violence depicted in Revelation 6-16 is literal violence in the real world, but a visionary scene expressed in metaphorical language. For example, "The sword and fire by which the evil of the earth is judged (and even 'tormented') are not literal swords and fire but metaphors for the cutting, searing *word* (1:16, 11:5)."[6]

John's violent and judgmental imagery "is the insider language of the confessing community expressing praise and gratitude for salvation," Boring notes, not just vindictive.[7]

4. John's theology and purpose

John's use of violent imagery reveals his conviction that humans (including Christians) are universally sinful and rightfully subject to judgment.

In Christ, however, traditional images are transformed. The lion becomes the lamb. Vengeance becomes self-sacrifice. Jesus is clad in bloody garments, but the blood is his own (1:5, 19:13).

God's purpose is that all may be saved. "While the world may reel under the hammer blows of God's wrath, it is also redeemed and released from the power of Satan (20:1-6)."[8]

Thus, while the bloody imagery of Revelation is awful, it is also awe-full, not a vindictive screed but a visionary and metaphorical attempt to assure John's readers of the power and presence of God.

NOTES

[1]Eugene Boring, *Revelation*, Interpretation: A Bible Commentary for Teaching and Preaching (Louisville: KY: John Knox Press, 1989), 131.

[2]Albert Schweitzer, *Out of My Life and Thought* (New York: Henry Holt and Co., 1933), 279.

[3]Boring, *Revelation*, 113-119.

[4]Ibid., 114.

[5]Ibid., 116; compare Rev. 8:7 and 11:19 with Exod. 9:23-25, 19:18-19; Judg. 5:4-5; 1 Kgs. 19:11-13; Ps. 18:7-15; and others.

[6]Boring, *Revelation*, 116.

[7]Ibid.

[8]Ibid., 118.

Revelation 12:1-18

ENTER THE DRAGON

Rejoice then, you heavens and those who dwell in them!
But woe to the earth and the sea,
for the devil has come down to you with great wrath,
because he knows that his time is short!
—Revelation 12:12

Have you ever attended a play in which multiple vignettes are used to portray the same general story? While Act One may take place in a courthouse or living room, Act Two might be on a battlefield with different characters, but facing the same human challenge.

This is essentially what we find when the curtain rises over Revelation 12. By the end of ch. 11, wrath has been poured out on the wicked, the dead have been judged, God's servants have been rewarded, and God's heavenly home is filled with an uncountable number of saints. That would have been a good place to stop, but John has more to say. He does so by shifting his focus to a completely different scene in which he re-envisions and Christianizes a popular myth to tell essentially the same story in a different way.

A WOMAN, A BABY—AND A DRAGON
(vv. 1-6)

In the previous chapters, Christ is portrayed as dwelling victorious in heaven, symbolically described as a lamb with seven eyes, seven horns, and the marks of slaughter still upon him. With ch. 12, John narrates a flashback vision that recalls Jesus' birth, his victory, and the present state of the church—all in clearly mythological language, designed to relate familiar events from a heavenly or spiritual perspective. The ancients typically believed that earthly events had heavenly or spiritual counterparts. While the Gospels describe Jesus' incarnation, death, resurrection, and ascension from a human point of view, John offers a "behind the scenes" view of how it might have appeared from the perspective of spiritual beings. ♦

Powerful stories: All of the ancient societies known to John—Greeks, Romans, Persians, Babylonians, Egyptians, and Jews as well—told stories of conflict between the gods, often played out in the heavens. Dragons, women, and their defenders were common elements in the various accounts. The same basic myth was often revised for different cultures. One well-known story as adapted by the Greeks is reminiscent of John's account in Revelation 12:

In the story of Apollo's birth, the god Zeus impregnated the goddess Leto. It was prophesied that the child of their union would one day kill the dragon Python, so Python set out to kill both mother and child. The sea god Poseidon came to Leto's defense, transporting her to an island and sinking it beneath the sea. After Python gave up the chase, Poseidon brought the island back to the surface and Leto gave birth to Apollo—who grew up to chase down Python and kill him.

Some of the Roman emperors retold the story, portraying themselves as Apollo the conqueror and the city of Rome as their mother, the queen of heaven.

A familiar image: The child who is destined "to rule with a rod of iron" is an image drawn from Ps. 2:9, where it describes a king of Israel who has been adopted by God to rule the earth. The verse was popularly interpreted as a messianic prophecy, and the early church believed it was fulfilled in Christ.

The image of a woman in labor was sometimes used in the Old Testament as an image of Israel (Isa. 26:17-18, 66:7-9; Mic. 4:10). The woman described in Rev. 12:1 could be thought of as Mary in particular, or as the nation of Israel, from whom Christ was born, in general. Before the chapter ends, the woman will morph into the church, the community of God's faithful people. Mythical language allows John to inject multiple meanings into a single image.

Understanding John's use of metaphor and myth helps us to avoid the interpretive mistakes of (a) thinking this is a literal description of an actual event and (b) assuming that the events beginning with ch. 12 follow the previous chapters in a chronological sequence. Indeed, as a flashback to the Christ event, ch. 12 relates something that has already happened rather than something yet to come.

John describes "a great portent" in the heavens, where a woman floats into view. Robed with the sun, with the moon as her footstool and a crown of stars, the woman's appearance marks her as regal, like the queen of heaven (v. 1). The woman is crying out in the last throes of giving birth (v. 2), but is also in danger. A powerful monster hovers nearby, waiting to devour her child, who is destined "to rule the nations with a rod of iron."

John describes the creature as a red dragon with seven heads, ten horns, and seven crowns—symbols of chaos, power, and authority. ♦

With a flick of its tail, John says, the dragon swept a third of the stars from the sky and cast them down to the earth while waiting to devour the woman's child (v. 4). This is another reminder that the story consists of one metaphor after another. Today we know that even the smallest of stars are millions of times more massive than the earth: that a third of the stars in the universe could be thrown to the earth is ludicrous. Neither John nor his readers knew this: stars appeared to them as tiny objects that could fall to the earth with no ill effects. Like the story of creation in Genesis 1, John's language is mythical or metaphorical rather than scientific: the point is, that dragon is a powerful force to be reckoned with.

> ♦ **A multivalent dragon:** The dragon in John's story is more than an adaptation of the Greek Python alone. As Mitchell Reddish describes it: "This dragon is Python from the Leto myth; he is also Tiamat, the seven-headed monster of the deep in Babylonian mythology; as well he is Leviathan, the serpentlike monster in Hebrew folklore (cf. Ps 74:14); further, he is the deceitful serpent of the garden of Eden story; and he is also Satan, 'the deceiver of the whole world' (12:9). He is each of these—and all of them combined—for he is the representation of all that is evil and chaotic and in opposition to God."[1]

Despite that, the dragon failed in his effort to steal and eat the child, which was "snatched away and taken to God and to his throne," while the woman fled from the heavens to the wilderness, where God protected her for 1,260 days. That period is equivalent to three and a half years, equal to the "time, times, and half a time" that John had adopted from Daniel's apocalypse, which predicted a similar period of trial for the Jews who suffered under Antiochus Epiphanes (vv. 5-6, 14; cf. Dan. 7:25, 12:7).

John's vision, then, is a much abbreviated and metaphorical account of the gospel: Jesus was born of mother Israel, overcame evil threats against him, and ascended to the throne room of heaven.

MICHAEL AND THE DRAGON
(vv. 7-12)

With v. 7, John switches gears again, backing up to give an account suggesting how the child was saved from the dragon. A belief had developed in Judaism that God's creation included any number of angels, some more powerful than others, with archangels being leaders of the lesser angelic hosts. Various archangels were thought to have responsibility for particular areas or peoples. An archangel named Michael was considered to be the patron protector of the Hebrews.

Thus, we are not surprised when John says that Michael led his angelic warriors to do battle with the dragon and his minions, defeating the dragon and casting him down to the earth (vv. 7-8). In v. 9 he gives the dragon a name: "that ancient serpent, who is called the Devil and Satan, the deceiver of the whole world." The concept of Satan as a spiritual being opposed to God is not present in the Old Testament, but developed in Judaism late, during the Second Temple period. 🔯

The dragon's power to harm the child had been blunted, as John heard a great voice from heaven proclaim that the salvation of God through the power of the Messiah had been achieved. Apocalyptic writing often imagined that earthly struggles had heavenly counterparts, and that is the case here. Michael's victory over the dragon in the heavens corresponded to Jesus' victory over evil through his crucifixion and resurrection. Although the dragon remained active on earth and continued to accuse the Messiah's kindred (Christ's followers), its heavenly aspirations had been conquered "by the blood of the Lamb" and by the testimony of the martyrs, "who did not cling to life even in the face of death" (vv. 10-11).

This view of Satan's defeat and the role of faithful witnesses is reflected in a different form by Luke 10:18, where Luke says that when the 70 who had been sent on mission returned, Jesus said "I watched Satan fall from heaven like a flash of lightning."

These words would have encouraged John's readers, some of whom faced death at the hands of the Roman beast (described in ch. 13) if they did not recant their faith in Christ. They needed such encouragement because the dragon was defeated, but not dead. He had been exiled to earth, where he had arrived "with great wrath, because he knows that his time is short" (v. 12).

This was John's way of explaining why Christians could trust a victorious Messiah and worship an all-powerful God but still face the tribulations of a world in which evil remains both present and active.

For Reflection: *Some readers may find it hard to get their heads around the idea that some scriptures are intentionally cast in the form of metaphor or myth. Can you see why John found such language to be a powerful and effective form of communicating hope to his Christian friends who suffered under Roman rule?*

⚓ **The rise of Satan:** The concept of Satan as portrayed in the New Testament and in folk theology is not present in the Old Testament. The tempter in Genesis 3 is not Satan, but a serpent—a creature "more crafty than any other wild animal the LORD God had made" (Gen. 3:1). In the book of Job, the adversary who wanted God to test Job was not called by a personal name, but by his title: *ha-satan* ("the accuser") was a member of God's inner council who served as a sort of heavenly district attorney.

The only time in the Old Testament that the word *satan* appears as a name, not prefaced by "the," is in 1 Chron. 21:1, which says that "Satan stood up against Israel, and incited David to count the people of Israel." This was a revised version of a story in 2 Samuel 24, which says "Again the anger of the LORD was kindled against Israel, and he incited David against them, saying 'Go, count the people of Israel and Judah'" (v. 1). The writer of Chronicles, written much later than 2 Samuel, was hesitant to say that God inspired David to do wrong, and so put it on Satan. Whether he still thought of Satan as a member of God's council sent to do the job, or whether he had begun to think of Satan as inimical to God, is unclear.

In late Judaism, after long exposure to the Persian and Greek concepts of good and evil gods, Jewish writings began to identify the serpent of Genesis 3 and the accuser of Job 1-2 as a powerful evil being opposed to God, called Satan. In popular thought, Satan became an evil power separate from God who ruled over the underworld and was served by his own angelic underlings, called demons. Jewish tradition called him by several names, including Belial and Azazel, adapted from the Old Testament inferences, along with Shemyaza, Mastema, and the Devil (Greek *diabolos*).

The concept of Satan became so widespread in Judaism that New Testament writers also adopted it as an explanation of how evil could become so powerful in the good world created by God, or a way to avoid attributing evil to God.

THE DRAGON AND THE WOMAN
(vv. 13-18)

With vv. 13-14, John again backs up, this time to say more about the woman's escape from the dragon. With both of them now on earth, the dragon pursued the woman, but she was given the wings of an eagle to fly into the wilderness and find safety for the "time, times, and half a time" described in v. 6 as 1,260 days, a motif borrowed from Daniel's prediction that the tribulations caused by Antiochus would last for three and a half years.

Modern readers typically think of dragons as breathing fire, but John says this dragon, unable to reach the woman, "poured water like a river after the woman, seeking to sweep her away with the flood" (v. 15). This time the earth itself came to her rescue, absorbing the water so the woman remained safe (v. 16). ⬥

Unable to harm the woman, the dragon turned its ire against her other children: it "went off to make war on the rest of her children, those who keep the commandments of God and hold the testimony of Jesus" (v. 16).

Chapter 12 ends with the dragon "taking a stand by the seashore," where it witnessed the arrival of two beasts. The first was a horrific hodgepodge of animal parts clearly designed to represent the Roman Empire (and its emperor), which was given power to utter blasphemies by demanding emperor worship, and granted authority to wage war against the people of God (13:1-10).

The second beast, lesser than the first, appears to represent the government officials charged with carrying out the emperor's demand to be worshiped and to dominate life by permeating the land with his mark, probably a reference to the emperor's image and claims to divinity being imprinted on coins used to buy and sell goods (13:11-18).

Here it becomes clear that John is drawing a metaphorical picture of a present reality rather than end-times events: although Christ proved victorious over evil through his death and resurrection, evil was still alive and active on the earth. Christ's followers were still subject to attack and tribulation through those who imposed the emperor cult. All was not lost, however.

In the face of severe trial and the threat of death for remaining true to Christ, believers could willingly die for their faith, believing that there was a place for them around God's throne and that "the word of their testimony" as martyrs played an ongoing role in defeating the power of evil. They

---

⬥ **Exodus imagery:** We have noted that the woman appears to be symbolic of both Israel, through whom Christ was born, and the church, which follows Christ. Two elements of the story in vv. 13-16 contain images that recall Israel's experience in the Exodus, when the people escaped from Egypt to find refuge in the wilderness.

As the earth swallowed up the flood sent out by the pursuing dragon (vv. 15-16), the Israelites had escaped Pharaoh's pursuit when God parted the sea that appeared to have trapped them (Exodus 14). When the people arrived at Sinai, God told Moses to declare to them "You have seen what I did to the Egyptians, and how I bore you on eagles' wings and brought you to myself" (Exod. 19:4)—an event recalled in the woman of Revelation 12 being given eagle's wings to fly into the wilderness (v. 14).

could be confident, believing the promise declared in the hopeful interlude of ch. 14: "And I heard a voice from heaven saying, 'Write this: Blessed are the dead who from now on die in the Lord.' 'Yes,' says the Spirit, 'they will rest from their labors, for their deeds follow them.'"

For Reflection: *Can you think of a time when you were challenged to recant your faith or, at least, to keep it hidden? Social situations and peer pressure may tempt us to keep our faith and values under wraps. More seriously, we sometimes read of Christians being kidnapped by religious extremists and brutally executed if they do not convert. Have you ever considered how you would respond in such a situation? Would the teaching of Revelation offer you any encouragement or consolation?*

THE HARDEST QUESTION
Should we still talk about "Satan" in personal terms?

We have explained above that the concept of Satan developed late in Judaism, and was adopted by the early church, which grew out of Judaism and flourished within a Greek and Roman culture with a long tradition of good and evil gods.

Is it still appropriate to talk about Satan in personal terms today? Mitchell Reddish suggests several reasons why imagining a personal, demonic Satan could still be helpful—or not. First, he suggests, speaking of Satan in personal terms may help us to remember that evil is serious business, and not overlook the pervasiveness, power, and attraction of evil in society.

Second, Reddish points out, Satan language reminds us that evil is more than just bad choices by an individual, or the collective evil of all hurtful actions. There is a systemic dimension of evil that affects organizational, political, or even religious systems, turning them from positive to negative forces. Like John's vision of a many-headed dragon, evil comes from different directions and persists even when one manifestation is exposed or defeated. Thinking of evil as Satanic may help us appreciate how pervasive it is.

Even so, there are decided downsides to imagining Satan as an evil, powerful, supernatural being. Doing so sets up a dualistic system of dueling gods. The Bible clearly teaches that there is only one God, but the popular view of Satan portrays him as an alternate deity who acts as God's archenemy. The notion that Satan is an angel gone rogue who was thrown out of heaven and then grew in power to rival God is not biblical at all. For example, the much-misunderstood account of "Lucifer" being cast out of heaven is an obvious misinterpretation of Isaiah 14, in which Isaiah celebrated the death of a Babylonian king who had proudly thought of himself in divine terms as the morning star.

"Lucifer," a Latin term that means "light-bearer," is a poor translation of a term meaning "daystar" that goes back to the Vulgate and was followed by later translations. A late Jewish tradition in the apocryphal book of 1 Enoch 6-36 is an unfortunate expansion of the story in Gen. 6:1-4 that claims certain "sons of God" chose to come to earth and have sex with human women, giving rise to giants. The popular notion of Satan as a prideful angel who was cast out of heaven owes its existence to John Milton's *Paradise Lost*, not to the Bible (Milton's account is in Book 1, lines 34-49).

To speak of Satan as a rival to God steps backward from biblical monotheism and adopts a theologically dualistic system more at home in Zoroastrianism than Christianity. Any view that allows for multiple gods fails to recognize the singularity of God.

Another risk in identifying evil with a personal Satan is perhaps more dangerous to our spiritual health, for it tempts us to blame the devil for our wrongdoing rather than accepting personal responsibility for the evil in our lives. The much-practiced art of "passing the buck" has been around as long as humans have lived on the earth. The Bible illustrates this with the story of Adam and Eve, who accepted the serpent's word over God's and chose to eat from a forbidden tree. When God called them to account, the man blamed his actions on "the woman that you gave me," implicating both the woman and God as more guilty than he. The woman then blamed the serpent, who—as jokesters sometimes note—didn't have a leg to stand on.

We cannot blame our evil on our parents, our peers, our culture—or on Satan. When we choose to do evil, the guilt lies in our own minds and hearts. As long as we can point an accusing finger at Satan to evade culpability for our own doings, we see no need to change our ways or behave more responsibly—or even to demand that corporations or culture as a whole should own up to institutional sins. Blaming Satan is a step backward from maturity and growth for both individuals and society.

Yet another problem, Reddish suggests, is that using Satan language may prompt us to demonize or "satanize" people or institutions that we believe act in opposition to God. If we think of others as being possessed by demons or under satanic control, we are less likely to have compassion for them, and more likely to feel good about harming them.

A final danger relative to characterizing evil as an incarnate Satan is that such an approach may lead us to trivialize evil, failing to appreciate the power it can have over us. When we think of Satan as a pitchfork-toting devil in red tights, or as a cartoonish demon whispering temptations into our ears, we're less likely to recognize how dangerous evil really is.

Reddish concludes: "If continuing to speak of evil in terms of Satan helps one to realize and confront the reality of rebelliousness, corruption, and failure in the world, then Satan language has a place for the modern Christian. On the other hand, if one finds such language repugnant and not useful, then one should find other images and concepts that communicate the reality that Satan language was intended to express. Belief in a personal, metaphysical being called Satan is not a required doctrine of the Christian faith."[2]

NOTES

[1]Mitchell G. Reddish, Revelation, *Smyth & Helwys Bible Commentary* (Macon, GA: Smyth & Helwys, 2001), 234.

[2]For a fuller discussion, see Reddish, *Revelation*, 240-248.

R

Revelation 17:1-18

ALAS, BABYLON . . .

The woman you saw is the great city that rules over the kings of the earth.
—Revelation 17:8

When modern readers come to the book of Revelation, some find its bloody judgments and outlandish imagery to be fascinating, while others perceive it to be troubling and distasteful, at least in certain aspects. One of these is John's portrayal of the earth's premier source of wickedness as a woman, and not just as a woman, but one described in the most unflattering of terms: she is a gaudy and drunken whore who keeps company with unsavory characters and is ultimately torn apart by them.

We live in a time and culture that is more sensitive to the immense capabilities and fully deserved rights of women to function as equals in society. We rightly decry sexist attitudes that devalue women and contribute to situations in which girls and women are abused. Is there any place in our time for a text that seems to border on misogyny?

As always in biblical studies, we must remember that the texts are products of their own culture and time. Even in our own day, novels and movies can portray women as both powerful heroines or evil villains, so perhaps we should not be too troubled that John could admire the sun-draped mother of ch. 12 and disparage the beast-riding harlot of ch. 17. Both are symbols: the woman in ch. 12 appears as a queen of heaven, one who represents both the people of Israel through whom Christ was born and the people of faith who Christ redeemed. The woman of ch. 17 sits enthroned as an earthly ruler who personifies the power of Rome, a monarch whose immorality represents both pagan worship and human greed.

As distasteful as she might be to our modern sensitivities, the metaphorical woman of Rev. 17:1–19:10 is deserving of a closer look.

A WOMAN AND A CITY
(vv. 1-2)

The opening of ch. 17 follows John's vision of seven horrifying bowls of divine wrath being poured out on a wicked world, and is connected to it by John's comment that his guide for the following vision is "One of the seven angels who had the seven bowls" (v. 1). The expansive vision of 17:1–19:10 appears to be an enlarged picture or alternate description of the seventh bowl judgment (16:17-21), in which a catastrophic earthquake led to the destruction of "the great city" of Babylon and "the cities of the nations."

This reminds us that Revelation has a convoluted chronology: visions overlap, flash back, or reprise events such as the fall of Rome, telling and retelling the story in different ways. The book was never intended to provide a linear time-line of future events, but an unmistakable insistence that God will ultimately be victorious.

In Revelation, the name Babylon appears frequently as a thinly veiled refer-ence to Rome, both the city and the Roman Empire it stands for, sometimes embodied in the person of the emperor. As is typical of apocalyptic literature, the symbols are fluid and multiple: a single symbol may have more than one mean-ing, while multiple symbols may represent the same reality.

John's reference to one of the "bowl" angels in vv. 1-2 serves to introduce a block of text that extends through 19:10. The woman appears first in ch. 17, and her judgment is announced. The judgment is revisited in ch. 18, and is referred back to in 19:1-10. ♦

♦ An interpreting angel:

In other examples of apocalyptic literature, it is common for an angel guide to accompany the writer on his visionary journeys and to inter-pret what he sees. Although John begins his book with a notice that God had sent an angel to him (1:1), ch. 17 marks the first place where an angel speaks up to interpret what John is seeing. An angel guide will also show John around the New Jerusalem in 21:9–22:9, but doesn't offer any explanations there.

While Revelation is rife with symbolic metaphors, few of them are portrayed as being overtly allegorical. The interpretation of the image in vv. 1-6 is one of few exceptions (see also 1:9-20 and 10:8-10).

The angel's invitation, "Come, and I will show you," is a common method of introducing a new vision in which the author is "carried away" in a trance to some distant place: in v. 3 John speaks of being "carried away in the spirit into a wilderness." The angel promises to show him "the judgment of the great whore who is seated on many waters, with whom the kings of the earth have committed fornication, and with the wine of whose fornication the inhabitants of the earth have become drunk" (vv. 1b-2).

Portraying wayward people or cities as metaphorical prostitutes was common in the Old Testament, especially with reference to pagan cities such as Tyre (Isa. 23:16-17) and Nineveh (Nah. 3:4), but also to a faithless Jerusalem (Isa. 1:21) or an idolatrous nation (Jer. 3:6-10; Ezek. 16:15-22, 23:1-49; Hos. 4:12-13, 5:3). John's apocalypse is rife with Old Testament allusions, and this is one of them.

The angel's description of the "great whore" as being "seated on many waters" could fit either the city of Babylon, which was surrounded by canals and bisected by the river Euphrates, or Rome, which was built on the banks of the Tiber River. The angel interpreted the "many waters" on which the woman sits as "peoples and crowds and nations and languages" who lived under Roman domination (v. 15), again drawing on Old Testament images such as Ps. 144:7; Isa. 8:6-7, 17:12-14, 28:17; and Jer. 47:2.

The woman's alleged "fornication" with "the inhabitants of the earth" is probably a reference to Rome's political alliances with client kingdoms throughout the empire, who have become "drunk" (and thus both impaired and complicit) through their relations with her.

> **For Reflection:** *Why do you think John's vision uses the metaphor of illicit sexual behavior to describe the relation between Rome's rulers and the client kings or others who profited from their support of the empire?*

THE WOMAN AND THE BEAST
(vv. 3-6)

The image shifts with v. 3: the woman is no longer seated on many waters, but on the back of a frightful beast, scarlet in color and covered with "blasphemous names." We have met this beast before: in ch. 13 it emerged from the water to serve the red dragon, which also had seven heads and ten horns. In 13:1, as here, John says the beast is covered with "blasphemous names." It soon becomes clear that the beast represents various facets of the Roman Empire, its capital, and its emperor, so it is likely that the "blasphemous names" reflect the various emperors' penchant for ascribing to themselves divine appellatives such as "lord and god" or "savior," an act both Jews and Christians would consider to be sacrilegious.

The woman who sits on the beast like a queen on her throne is dressed in expensive garments of scarlet and purple, adorned with "gold and jewels and pearls" (v. 4a). One might assume the intention is to portray her as royalty, but it is more likely that she is meant to appear in gaudy if opulent dress, flaunting the wealth gained through her unsavory but profitable occupation. ☝

The golden cup in the woman's hand adds to her ostentatious image. It is filled, not with wine, but with "abominations and the impurities of her fornication" (v. 4b). The image is awkward, but calls to mind the Romans' support of pagan religious practices, some

☝ **Woman or city?** In Rev. 17:5, John depicts the woman sitting on the beast as being richly clothed and draped with jewels. In 18:16, a later part of the same vision, he describes "the great city" of Rome in similar terms: "clothed in fine linen, in purple and scarlet, adorned with gold, with jewels, and with pearls!" He can do this because the woman is not to be thought of as a literal person, but as a visionary metaphor for the city.

of which might include immoral aspects such as cultic prostitution. It could also be a swipe at the imperial cult, which required residents to pay homage to the emperor, an action that Jews and Christians alike considered to be idolatrous. ☝

To the unflattering portrayal of the woman's sumptuous apparel and flamboyant jewelry, John adds that a name was written across her forehead: "Babylon the great, mother of whores and of earth's abominations" (v. 5). In Revelation, Babylon is a code name for Rome, which John sees as the epicenter of idolatry and immorality throughout the world. Several cities in Asia Minor boasted temples to *Dea Roma* (the goddess of Rome), and the emperor cult was practiced to varying degrees wherever the empire's tentacles reached. The motif of having an identifying mark or label on the forehead is com-

☝ **John and Jeremiah:** The description of the woman's golden cup of abominations that makes the nations drunk (17:5-6) is reminiscent of Jer. 51:7, which portrays Babylon as a golden cup in Yahweh's hand, making the rest of the earth drunk with the wine of divine judgment.

mon in Revelation, signifying either one's alliance with God (3:12, 7:3, 9:4, 14:1, 19:12, 22:4) or with the beast (13:16-18).

One might expect the woman to have become inebriated from the idolatrous contents of her cup, but John says instead that she is "drunk with the blood of the saints and the blood of the witnesses to Jesus" (v. 6). Believers who refused to worship the emperor often paid the price for their faithfulness with blood.

John's response of amazement at what he has seen, common in apocalyptic visions, opens the door for the angel to interpret the allegorical significance of the vision.

> **For Reflection:** *In Revelation, the faithful were marked with God's "seal" on their foreheads, while followers of the beast bore its identifying mark. Can you think of contemporary illustrations of ways in which we demonstrate allegiance to God, country, or even sports teams through apparel or even body markings?*

THE WOMAN'S COMING JUDGMENT
(vv. 7-18)

"I will tell you the mystery," the angel said, "of the woman, and of the beast with seven heads and ten horns that carries her" (v. 7). The beast, he said, "was, and is not, and is about to ascend from the bottomless pit and go to destruction" (v. 8a). ♆ In the latter part of the verse he again referred to the beast as one who "was and is not and is to come" (v. 8b). A few verses later, he said the beast "was and is not, it is an eighth but it belongs to the seven, and it goes to destruction" (v. 11).

Do we need our own interpreting angel to make sense of this? The description of the beast as one who "was and is not and is to come" is clearly intended as a parody or contrast to John's earlier descriptions of God as "him who is and who was and who is to come" (1:4, 8), and as "the Lord God Almighty, who was and is and is to come" (4:8). God has never ceased to exist, and is poised for a future coming in judgment. The beast represents someone who had lived and died, and who John expected to return in an eschatological role. ♆

> ♆ **Ascending from the abyss:** The reference to the beast "about to ascend from the bottomless pit" in v. 8 is very similar to 11:7, which speaks of "the beast that comes up from the bottomless pit." In both cases, "bottomless pit" translates the Greek word *abussos*, the root of the English word "abyss."
>
> The term apparently refers to the netherworld, the world of the dead, which the ancients thought existed beneath the earth, both land and sea. Thus, the reference to the beast "rising out of the sea" in 13:1 does not suggest that it was a sea creature, but that it has come up from the land of the dead, rising through the sea.

⚓ **The beast**: The beast as a narrative character makes multiple appearances in Revelation. Its arrival is predicted in 11:7, it first appears in 13:1-8, and it is described more fully in 17:3-17. The account of the beast's defeat in 17:13-14 is retold in more detail in 19:17-21. Several other texts make reference to the brand-like "mark of the beast" or to demands that people worship its image (14:9, 15:2, 16:2). In other references, the beast's throne is the target of the fifth bowl of wrath (16:10); foul froglike spirits come from its mouth after the sixth bowl is poured out (16:13); and it is later consigned to torment in a lake of fire and sulfur (20:10).

The seven heads of the beast are given two meanings—unusual in apocalyptic but a reminder of how fluid symbolism can be. On the one hand, the seven heads represent the seven mountains of Rome, the angel explained (v. 9a). But they also represent seven kings, "of whom five have fallen, one is living, and the other has not yet come, and when he comes, he must remain only a little while" (vv. 9b-10). This is apparently a reference to a sequence of emperors, five of whom "had fallen" (most did not die peacefully), one of whom was still ruling, and one who was yet to assume the throne for a short-lived reign. After that, John anticipated that the beast—identified in v. 11 as an eighth head that also belongs to the seven—would return to power, unite ten ascendant kings (the ten horns described in v. 12), and go to war with the Lamb (Jesus), who would defeat them (vv. 13-14). ⚓

The puzzling description of the beast as "an eighth who belongs to the seven" is probably a cryptic reference to Nero, who ruled from 54-68 CE and had shown

⚓ **Who were the kings?** One would think that by identifying which seven kings/emperors John has in mind, we could easily date the book—or that if we knew the date, we could determine which seven emperors he was describing. This is a far more difficult task than it appears.

Some emperors ruled for such a short time that even Roman historians tended to discount them as real emperors. Any good commentary on Revelation will include comparative charts that explain how difficult it is to determine where to begin and end with the seven. One thing we can be fairly certain about is that Nero would be one of the earlier kings, as he is "an eighth, but it belongs to the seven" (17:11).

Some writers have attempted a purely historic approach to the problem, while others take a more symbolic view and yet others combine the two. It is entirely possible that John doesn't intend to specify any seven particular rulers, but is using seven as an apocalyptic symbol of completion.

particular cruelty to Christians in Rome. Within Roman society, a *Nero Redivivus* myth held that Nero would rise from the dead and rule again: John's vision apparently reflects that popular belief in imagining the beast as the villainous Nero who would return from the dead and lead an unsuccessful war against Jesus.

Jumping back to the initial image of the woman seated on the waters (v. 1, before she was seated on a beast in the wilderness), the angel interprets the waters as "peoples and multitudes and nations and languages," a probable reference to the various populations who lived under Roman domination.

Readers who expect a neat chronology in Revelation will be disappointed to note that vv. 16-17 describe events that would have occurred before vv. 13-14. The *Nero Redivivus* myth expected Nero redux to turn against Rome and lead a coalition of Parthian kings to defeat and destroy his former empire. In a similar vein, John's vision sees the revived beast uniting the ten kings (its ten horns) and then turning against its rider, making the woman "desolate and naked" by plundering her riches before they "devour her flesh and burn her with fire."

The woman's frightening fate at the hands of the turncoat kings would come about as a result of God's initiative, the angel insisted, "for God has put it into their hearts to carry out his purpose" by joining the beast in ravaging Rome. And, lest there be any misunderstanding that Rome is the intended target, he adds: "the woman you saw is the great city that rules over the earth" (v. 18).

Here at the end of the chapter, we return to our initial question: Can we profit from a text that portrays an evil and idolatrous empire in the form of an immoral woman? Other texts in Revelation similarly portray feminine sexuality in a negative way, such as the "Jezebel" of 2:20-23 who led others into adultery with her, and the 144,000 faithful "who have not defiled themselves with women" (14:4). Domineering men might call on texts such as this to reinforce a belief in male superiority or to justify mistreatment of women, while some women might find their own self-image eroded through reading the same accounts: language and imagery are powerful forces.

How do we avoid reading biblical texts in damaging ways? One tempting option is simply to ignore the texts that offend us, but in doing so we run the risk of failing to hear a word God wants us to understand. A better option is to remind ourselves of the ancients' cultural context and seek ways to re-imagine the text in imagery that speaks more clearly within our own life setting.

The intent of John's vision is to encourage fearful Christians whose very lives were threatened by idolatrous emperors and their power-hungry minions. The visions declare in no uncertain terms that the empire's days are numbered, the Lamb will defeat the beast, and the righteous can look forward to a glorious future.

For Reflection: *Can you think of alternate metaphors for the imagery in this vision? Could you imagine a heartless dictator in place of the woman, perhaps, or a greedy financial conglomerate in the role of the beast? What images would you suggest?*

THE HARDEST QUESTION
Had John seen the image of his vision on a coin?

Careful readers will note that vv. 1-6 of Revelation 17 are are different from most visions in Revelation because the imagery is static: a woman sits above many waters, or on a beast, but there is no movement or action. Some scholars have suggested that the image John describes in these verses could have been inspired by a prominent piece of artwork portraying Rome as a woman seated on seven hills above the Tiber River.

John's description is quite similar to that of a coin known as a *sestertius* that was minted during Vespasian's rule (69-79 CE). The front of the coin carries the image of Vespasian, along with his name, titles, and indications that the coin was minted with the authorization of the Roman senate.

The back side of the coin is more interesting. It depicts the patron goddess of Rome (*Dea Roma*) seated on the city's famous seven hills, with the river god Tiber beside her right foot and the mythical she-wolf who nursed Romulus

The *Dea Roma* coin

(the mythical founder of Rome) and Remus below. This recalls the image in 17:1-6 in which a woman sits first above the waters, and then upon a beast whose seven heads represent the seven hills of Rome. David Aune describes this as a literary type called an *ekphrasis*, and suggests that the image on the coin was a copy of a well-known but no-longer extant work of art that the author of Revelation might have seen.[1]

NOTE

[1]David Aune, *Revelation 17-22*, Word Biblical Commentary, vol. 52c (Nashville: Thomas Nelson, 1998), 919-22.

Revelation

NO MORE TEARS

And the one who was seated on the throne said,
"See, I am making all things new."
—Revelation 21:1-6

Heaven: it's not a place most people think about very much until we get very sick or until someone close to us dies, and then it is all we can think about.

The truth is, we have no real idea what heaven is like, though our imagination runs wild, and the images we have from Revelation are not much help. In the first place, John's apocalyptic writing is highly metaphorical and symbolic, so we should not regard his language-stretching vision of jeweled walls and pearly gates and golden streets as a literal description of heaven, but as a place of beauty beyond our wildest imagination.

Secondly, what John describes in Revelation 21-22 is pointedly denoted as a "new heaven and a new earth." Whatever heaven might be like now, John suggests, it is not the same place or dimension that believers will enjoy in eternity. What the present heaven and the new heaven have in common is that God is at the heart of them.

The Bible does not tell us all we *want* to know about heaven, but it tells us all we *need* to know. It tells us that we can hold to the hope that life for the believer does not end with death, but continues with joy.

A NEW DWELLING
(v. 1-2)

As we come to Revelation 21-22, the terrifying visions of the previous chapters have come to an end. In various ways, John's apocalyptic visions declared a firm belief that the righteous might suffer and die, but God would conquer and banish all that is evil, opening the way to a new age of peace for God and God's people.

🔱 **Boiled in oil?** An early church tradition, recorded in Tertullian's "The Prescription of/ against Heretics," claims that John was dipped in boiling oil before a Roman audience, but was miraculously unharmed. Supposedly all who witnessed the event were converted to Christianity, and since the Romans couldn't kill John, they shipped him off to Patmos.

While there is no evidence to support this unlikely legend, there is little question that John must have experienced and witnessed the kind of severe persecutions that typically gave rise to apocalyptic writings.

We can imagine that heaven had been on John's mind for a long time. He had experienced persecution. No doubt he had lost friends to death in some of the more severe outbreaks, and had heard of others. Sporadic episodes of persecution reportedly included public torture, with Christians being burned as torches or fed to the lions in the Coliseum. One early church legend says that Roman officials tried to kill John, but could not, and so they just banished him to the island of Patmos. 🔱

It is easy to see why John thought so much about heavenly things. The Hebrew Bible testifies that God created the earth so that everything was "very good" (Gen. 1:31), but that humankind turned against God's way and misused the earth, leaving it cursed (Genesis 3).

When injustice reigned or enemies threatened and the situation looked particularly bad, the prophets sometimes spoke of a new or renewed earth where closeness to God would be restored. Isaiah of Jerusalem envisioned a new age of peace in which all creation would live in harmony with God (Isaiah 11), and a later prophet writing in Isaiah's name predicted an entirely new creation: "For I am about to create new heavens and a new earth; the former things shall not be remembered or come to mind" (Isa. 65:17).

John was certainly familiar with these ancient hopes, and he believed they were about to be fulfilled. "Then I saw a new heaven and a new earth," he said, "for the first heaven and the first earth had passed away, and the sea was no more" (v. 1).

John was convinced that God would soon draw earthly history to a close and set everything right. All that had become cursed and crooked would be restored and made straight as the earth was reborn and made new. The reasons for a new heaven are less obvious, but the ancients often thought of the two together. "A new heaven and a new earth" is John's way of emphasizing God's creative power to make all things new.

A new heaven and earth would be necessary, John said, because the old heaven and earth "have passed away." In the previous chapter, while describing the last judgment in which God would sit on a great white throne, John said "the earth and the heaven fled from his presence, and no place was found for them" (Rev. 20:11b).

Of special significance is John's insistence that "the sea was no more." The sea was a prominent source of fear in the ancient world. Maritime travel was dangerous and uncertain. Sea dragons or serpent-like monsters such as Leviathan were thought to inhabit the depths (Job 26:12; Isa. 27:1, 51:9-10), making the sea a fearful place. The sea symbolized chaos and the threatening power of un-creation, which could only be held in check by God. In the new heaven and earth, the sea would be no more. ♆

In addition to a new heaven and earth, John's vision included a new Jerusalem: "and I saw the holy city, the new Jerusalem, coming down out of heaven from God, prepared as a bride adorned for her husband" (v. 2).

The Jerusalem of old was the city of David, the home of the temple, the heart of every major religious festival. But it was also a city that could stone prophets and crucify Jesus. Luke's gospel speaks of how Jesus wept for the recalcitrant people of Jerusalem (Luke 13:31-35). Perhaps the new Jerusalem's descent from heaven is a reminder that only God can restore the city's holiness and transform it into a dwelling place fit for eternity.

♆ **No more sea:** The overwhelming and destructive power of the sea contributed to its association with chaos. No human could hope to control the sea, and few gods were thought to have such power. In the Babylonian creation myth, the god Marduk proved his supremacy by battling and defeating the sea-dwelling goddess Tiamat in order to stabilize the world and create humankind.

In Hebrew thought, the sea could also suggest separation from God. In the biblical concept of a "three-story" universe, the flat earth was covered by a dome-like "firmament" that held back the great cosmic sea above, with heaven thought to be beyond the sea. In the temple of Solomon, a huge container of water about 15 feet across stood between worshipers and the holy place. It was called "the bronze sea" (or "molten sea," 1 Kgs. 7:23-26). It may have been used for purification rites, but may also have indicated separation from God, or God's command over the sea.

In John's first vision of heaven (Rev. 4:6), the throne of God seemed to be set beyond "something like a sea of glass, like crystal." But in the new heaven and the new earth, there is no more sea. Chaos is no longer a threat. There is nothing to separate us from God.

⊕ **A bride adorned:** John has previously used imagery of a metaphorical marriage between Christ and his bride (Rev. 19:7-8). Now, he pictures the new Jerusalem "as a bride adorned for her husband." The perfect union of Christ and his bride is about to take place, but only God can fully prepare the bride for this moment.

Other New Testament passages use the wedding metaphor to describe the relationship of Christ and the church (2 Cor. 11:2), and Jesus himself once told a wedding parable about the kingdom of God in which being properly dressed was a significant issue (Matt. 22:1-14).

At first (and maybe, at last), this text seems confusing, but remember that John's vision is not a literal description. Apocalyptic visions such as these characteristically employ word pictures, metaphorical language that often shifts its boundaries. ⊕

John speaks of a new heaven and a new earth, with a new and holy city of Jerusalem coming down out of heaven to the new earth. After this, however, the distinctions fade, and the new heaven, earth, the city, and believers all seem to meld together. The new Jerusalem is not only a city but also the bride of Christ, the body of believers.

Surely the author does not intend for the reader to think that in eternity the faithful will live on earth while God lives in heaven. The whole point is that, in the new age, God's dwelling will be with God's people.

For Reflection: *What comes to mind when you think of dwelling in God's presence? Is it a frightening thought, or comforting?*

A NEW PRESENCE
(vv. 3-4)

John describes a loud voice from the throne saying, "See, the home of God is among mortals. He will dwell with them as their God; they will be his peoples, and God himself will be with them; he will wipe every tear from their eyes. Death will be no more; mourning and crying and pain will be no more, for the first things have passed away."

Here is the most important aspect of John's message. What the new heaven and new earth look like or where they are located or how big they are is immaterial. God will live among God's people: that is what truly matters.

That God's "tent" or "dwelling" would be among mortals is an incredible concept. To imagine God's presence, we will no longer need a tabernacle or an altar, the Ark of the Covenant or the holy of holies, a cross on a steeple or stained glass windows. Rather, God will dwell among us in some way beyond our present ability to imagine. The covenant relationship so longed for between God and Israel will finally be fulfilled (Exod. 6:7, Lev. 26:12, Jer. 7:23). ⚓

Living in the full presence of God will mean living in the absence of death, John says. Mourning and crying and pain, in one way or another, have a connection with death—the death of relationships, the death of dreams, the death of innocence, the death of trust, the death of loved ones, the death of good health, the death of self. Death, in some form, is at the heart of every pain.

The Bible has nothing good to say about death. ⚓ That's why it is such good news to hear that God will do away with it. Without the deathly fear of darkness and separation, there is no more cause for mourning or tears or pain. The ultimate sign of the presence of God is the absence of death.

⚓ **God's dwelling:** The word translated as "home" in the NRSV can also be rendered as "dwelling" (NIV) or "tabernacle" (KJV, NASB). The Greek word is *skene*, which literally means "tent." When the author of John's gospel claimed that "the Word became flesh and dwelt among us," he used the verbal form of the same word (lit., "tabernacled").

Skene is probably derived from a Semitic loan word such as the Hebrew *shakan* (to dwell), which gave rise to words such as *mishkan* (tent, tabernacle) and *shekinah* (dwelling). The rabbis often used the word *Shekinah* to refer to the very presence of God's glory thought to pervade the temple's most sacred space, the holy of holies.

⚓ **Death as an enemy:** Biblical accounts portray death coming into the world as an unwanted invader following humankind's sin (Genesis 3, Rom. 5:12), with the result that mortals became not only subject to death (Heb. 9:27), but also enslaved by the fear of it.[1]

The author of Ecclesiastes expresses great sorrow and frustration because he understood the ugliness and finality of death and saw nothing positive beyond. Isaiah looked forward to a day when death would be swallowed up forever (Isa. 25:8), and Paul announced that the longed-for day had come through the work of Christ (1 Cor. 15:54-56). Death, then, is seen as an enemy to be conquered, and "the last enemy to be destroyed is death" (1 Cor. 15:26).

This is precisely what John declares in Rev. 21:4.

For Reflection: *If you could meet one person in all of history, who would you choose? Albert Einstein? George Washington? Alexander the Great? King David? John says that one day we will not only meet but also live in the very presence of God. Try to picture what that would be like.*

A NEW WORD
(vv. 5-6)

God's final word is always a word of hope. "See, I am making all things new." The New Testament speaks of how Christians become a "new creation" when we trust in Christ and ask Christ's spirit to live in us (2 Cor. 5:17, Gal. 6:15). We do not become immediately perfect, but despite human weakness, we grow in the "inner person" as a new creation, secure in Christ until the day of his appearing (2 Cor. 3:18, 4:16-18, Col. 3:1-4). John now envisions this same transformation on a cosmic scale as all things are redeemed and made new.

G. B. Caird described John's vision of a corrupt world's miseries giving way to a future hope this way: "the agonies of earth are but the birth-pangs of a new creation."[2]

John declares God's own testimony that "these words are trustworthy and true" (v. 5). There will come a day when all the former things are past, when God, who is both beginning and end, will bring all things to an eternal conclusion in which the greatest needs of God's children are eternally met: "To the thirsty I will give water as a gift from the spring of the water of life" (v. 6).

John has more to say about the believer's eternal home (Rev. 21:7–22:21), but the most important thing has already been said. God is present. Death is absent. The noise of running water is not the sound of tears, but the eternally bubbling spring of the water of life.

THE HARDEST QUESTION
How do we interpret what seems to be impossible imagery?

Many of the images in Revelation are simply mind-boggling, and some of them seem impossible. How do we understand these things?

For example, Rev. 20:11b declares ". . . the earth and the heaven fled from his presence, and no place was found for them," while in 21:1 John says "Then I saw a new heaven and a new earth, for the first heaven and the first earth had passed away."

How could this be? Biblical writers had no concept of a universe such as we do, an unmeasurable space inhabited by uncounted galaxies containing multiplied billions of stars. For John, "heaven and earth" would represent all that existed—yet he declared that heaven and earth fled from God's presence.

As is typical of apocalyptic literature, we must remember that John is using word pictures, speaking in metaphorical language. Where could heaven and earth go apart from God? The psalmist testified that he could not flee from God's presence (Ps. 139:7). Could all of heaven and earth do so?

Similarly, John describes a new heaven, a new earth, and a new Jerusalem that appear to begin as separate entities, but they ultimately blend together. The elements of John's visions sometimes shift in their shape or meaning. At other times, multiple characters may represent the same evil power.

To understand this, think about how things work in our dreams: we may find ourselves moving instantly from one place to another, or discover that a classroom has turned into muddy marsh. Dreams often defy logic and morph from one thing to another, though we may learn something from the symbols that show up in them.

Perhaps it would be helpful for us to remember that John's revelations came to him in visions that he would have written later, and visions were very much like dreams thought to be sent from God.

NOTES

[1]Heb. 2:15, cf. Robert H. Mounce, *The Book of Revelation*, New International Commentary on the Old Testament (Grand Rapids: Eerdmanns, 1977), 372.

[2]G. B. Caird, *The Revelation of St. John the Divine* (New York: Harper & Row, 1966), 266.

R

Revelation 21:10–22:5

BETTER THAN YOU CAN IMAGINE

Then the angel showed me the river of the water of life,
bright as crystal, flowing from the throne of God and of the Lamb.
—Revelation 22:1

What's the most beautiful dwelling place you can imagine? A quaint cabin by a peaceful stream in a verdant forest? A downy bed with fluffy pillows in a luxury hotel? A private villa on the beach of a tropical island?

In Rev. 21:10–22:5, John does his best to describe the wonders and glories of the eternal dwelling place God will provide for God and for God's people, stretching the metaphor to the limit as he speaks of gigantic jewels, golden streets, verdant trees and a crystal river highlighting a new Jerusalem, an eternal dwelling place for God and for God's people.

THE CITY OF GOD
(21:9-21)

In the first part of Revelation 21, John described a new heaven and a new earth, with a new Jerusalem descending from heaven to rest on an earthly mountain—probably an idealized version of Mt. Zion (21:1-5). Note that the holy city "comes down from God out of heaven." This was necessary, some writers have noted, because humans proved entirely incapable of building such a holy city, a fit dwelling for God, on their own. It has to come from God, as a gift of grace.

It is also worth noting that this eternal dwelling of God and God's people, as described here, is *on earth*, albeit a new earth. We typically think of "going to heaven" in eternity, but John's terminology suggests that heaven comes to earth. ⬇

Like John, we would like to know more about this city, and as we continue reading, an angel comes to take John on a guided tour (21:10). The entire city

⚓ **A tale of two cities:** In earlier chapters, John gave considerable attention to the powerful city of Rome, thinly disguised as Babylon. Commentators
often note that John's description of the holy city is an intentional contrast to
the wicked city of Babylon/Rome. In Revelation 17-18, Babylon was described
as a sinful city located in the wilderness, a prostitute filled with abominations, a
dwelling of demons and place of death where kings come to practice "fornication" through their supportive relationship with Rome. John pictured it as a city
of darkness that deceives the nations and is ultimately destined for destruction.

In contrast, the new Jerusalem is a holy city located on a high mountain,
as the bride of the Lamb in which uncleanness and falsehood have no place. It
is the dwelling place of God, a setting of life where kings come to lay their glory
before God. This city is suffused with the light of God and heals the nations with
leaves from the tree of life, so that the redeemed might live there forever.

Just as the holy city described in 21:9-27 contrasts with the wicked city
pictured in chs. 17-18, the blissful picture imagined in chs. 21-22 should not be
separated entirely from the visions and judgment of ch. 20. When read entirely
apart, one may be tempted to focus on a deterministic millennialism (from ch.
20 alone) or an overly rosy assumption about what is to come (from ch. 21
alone). The message of Revelation includes judgment and grace, both death and
life, both despair and hope. It offers readers a choice about which destiny they
seek, and neither should be ignored.

glowed like clear jasper because of the presence of God (21:11), John said, with
12 gates arranged so that three were on each of the square city's four sides (21:12).
The gates, not inlaid with pearl but constructed from single massive pearls (21:21),
were inscribed with the names of the 12 tribes of Israel (21:14, 19-20).

The city rested on a foundation of 12 gigantic gemstones (21:14, 19-20) a
collection similar to the 12 jewels found on the high priest's breastplate in Exod.
28:15-20. A notable difference is that, while the gems in the priest's breastplate
were inscribed with the names of the 12 tribes of Israel, the enormous jewels on
which the new Jerusalem rested bore the names of the 12 apostles.

Some readers interpret this to mean that the church has supplanted Israel
and thus will inherit the promises once given to Israel, a view called "supersessionism" (for more on this, see "The Hardest Question" on page 70). It is
more likely that the vision portrays God's eternal dwelling as including those who
entered through both the old and the new covenants: while the foundation stones
bear the apostles' names, the 12 gates—where people enter the city—are named
for the 12 tribes of Israel.

The significance of the number 12 continues with the description of the holy city's size: the angel showed it to be shaped like a cube, measuring 12,000 stadia on each side. English translations range from 1400 to 1500 miles for this dimension, but the significant thing is not the precise size but the symbolism behind the number 12,000—another allusion to the 12 tribes and/or apostles. ♦

The number 12 again comes into play with John's assertion that the city's bright jasper wall measured "144 cubits," or about 72 yards (21:12, 17-18). Whether this refers to the height or the breadth of the wall is unclear: John doesn't say. A wall more than 70 yards high might seem immense to us, but it would appear insignificant outside of a city more than 1,400 miles tall. It is possible that John was referring to the width, but earlier he had described it as a "great, high wall" (21:12).

Again, the significance is in the numerical symbolism: 144 is the product of 12 times 12, perhaps another indication that both Israel (represented by the 12 tribes) and the church (represented by the 12 apostles) will have a role and a place when heaven comes to earth.

♦ **12,000 stadia:** The Roman *stade* (or *stadion*) was 600 Roman feet or about 100 double paces. The Roman foot was slightly longer than the American measure of a foot, and the *stade* is often said to be about 625 feet, or about one-eighth of a mile, though some estimates are longer. The NRSV translates 12,000 *stadia* as 1,500 miles; the NET translates this measure as 1,400 miles.

The word "stadium" originated from structures built for spectators to observe a straight-line foot race on a track one *stade* long.

♦ **Gold clear as glass:** The references to the walls and streets of the city being made of "pure gold, clear as glass" (21:18, 21) do not suggest some special type of gold that is transparent. Rather, the image is of gold so pure, unblemished, and shining that it reflects everything just as a perfect glass mirror would.

Many large cities have skyscrapers encased in gold-tinted glass that suggest the effect John has in mind.

The golden streets and bejeweled nature of the city calls to mind Isa. 54:11-12, where the prophet saw a day when God would secure the storm-tossed city of Jerusalem: "I am about to set your stones in antimony, and lay your foundations with sapphires. I will make your pinnacles of rubies, your gates of jewels, and all your wall of precious stones."

Their visionary materials and design are not an exact match, but both Isaiah and John saw the comforting image of a new Jerusalem built of the strongest, most imperishable, and most beautiful materials imaginable. ♦

For Reflection: *Does it bother you to think that John's visionary depiction of heaven is not intended as a literal description of a physical place? For example, would it trouble you to imagine that you could arrive in heaven without passing through pearly gates or walking down a street paved with gold?*

THE CITY OF LIGHT
(21:22-27)

John's description of the city bears many similarities to Ezekiel's apocalyptic writings, but v. 22 brings a sharp shift in emphasis. In Ezekiel's vision of a restored Jerusalem, the temple is the focal point of the city. In fact, the bulk of Ezekiel 40-48 is dedicated to an elaborate description of the renewed temple, its measurements, and its personnel.

John's vision of the new Jerusalem, however, has no temple at all, "for its temple is the Lord God Almighty and the Lamb" (21:22). The purpose of a temple in Israel, as throughout the ancient Near East, was to represent the dwelling place of the deity.

In the new Jerusalem, no temple is needed because the city itself is God's dwelling place, with the throne of God at its heart. In Ezekiel, "the glory of God filled the temple" (Ezek. 43:4-5), while for John the entire city is filled with God's glory (21:11).

As the city needs no temple, neither does it need the sun, the moon, nor lamps, because "the glory of God is its light, and its lamp is the Lamb" (21:23). This image recalls Isaiah's vision of a time when "The sun shall no longer be your light by day, nor for brightness shall the moon give light to you by night; but the LORD will be your everlasting light, and your God will be your glory" (Isa. 60:19; see also 60:1-2, 20).

Note John's careful and constant association of the Lamb (Christ) with God. The work of one is the work of the other: though he speaks of them in separate terms, John's image of deity includes both God (the Father) and the Lamb (Christ, the Son). ⛏

As a city of light, the new Jerusalem will attract the kings of the nations to bring their glory into it (21:24-26), even as Isaiah had predicted: "Nations shall come to your light, and kings to the brightness of your dawn" (Isa. 60:3, also 4-11).

⬥ **Where is the Holy Spirit?** Some readers may wonder why John is so careful to speak of both God and Christ the Lamb without also mentioning the Holy Spirit. It's important to remember that Trinitarian doctrine, as we know it today, was not fully developed until a few hundred years later. Still, there are images reflective of the Spirit's presence.

John's first vision of God's throne speaks of "seven spirits who are before his throne." When John first introduced Christ as the Lamb, he described the Lamb as having seven horns and seven eyes, "which are the seven spirits of God sent out into all the earth" (Rev. 5:6). The seven eyes/seven spirits appear as a rough approximation of the Holy Spirit, as they describe the pervasive Spirit of God throughout the world.

More particularly, the messages to the seven churches often include the phrase "listen to what the Spirit is saying to the churches" (2:7, 11, 17, 29; 3:6, 13, 22), even as the message is described as "the words of him who has the seven spirits of God and the seven stars" (3:1). In Rev. 22:17, the single imagery returns, as "the Spirit and the Bride say, 'Come.'"

So, though John doesn't use the terminology "Father, Son, and Holy Spirit," his language includes imagery related to all three.

John's reference to the nations bringing their glory before God may cause the careful reader some head-scratching, because previously in Revelation, the nations and their glory have had a negative connotation, resisting God and following the beast. Rev. 19:17-21 describes the destruction of the kings, and 20:7-9 pictures the destruction of the nations. Yet, they now come to present their glory to God. This appears as a paradox to us, but biblical literature, especially apocalyptic, is far less concerned with logical consistency than we typically expect.

Perhaps John has in mind the idea of nations or people who have come through the fire of destruction and been purified, as he notes that those who continue to practice "abomination or falsehood" will not be allowed into the city, only those "whose names are written in the Lamb's book of life" (21:27). Knowledge of when the Lamb's book will finally close to further enrollment is beyond our ken.

Some readers interpret this text, among others, to suggest that John believed in a universal salvation: that ultimately all people would be allowed to enter the holy city. Other passages indicate that people may choose a path that excludes them from God's presence, but John appears to harbor a hope that God's grace will ultimately overcome all human resistance.

THE RIVER OF LIFE
(22:1-5)

John's vision again recalls Ezekiel as the angel guide shows him "the river of the water of life, bright as crystal, flowing from the throne of God and of the Lamb through the middle of the street of the city" (22:1-2a).

Ezekiel had also described a river, one flowing from beneath the renewed temple, with lines of trees growing on either side (Ezek. 47:1-7). The river would bring life, for "Wherever the river goes, every living creature that swarms will live, and there will be very many fish, once these waters reach there. It will become fresh; and everything will live where the river goes" (Ezek. 47:9).

Moreover, the trees on either side of the river would bear fresh fruit every month, with their fruit offering food, "and their leaves for healing" (Ezek. 47:12).

The city of John's vision also features a "river of the water of life" pouring out from beneath the throne of God and the Lamb and flowing down the middle of the main street, with fruit-bearing trees on either side. ✋

As in Ezekiel's vision, the trees bear different kinds of fruit, producing crops year round that provide

✋ **Tree, or trees?** Translators struggle with Rev. 22:2, because the word for "tree" (*xulon*) in "tree of life" is singular, but John clearly says it is growing on both sides of the river, which flows down the middle of the street. The word *xulon* refers to wood in general: it can be used for firewood (which would likely be placed in stacks or bundles of individual pieces), and even though it is singular, it could be used in a collective sense to describe a grove or group of trees.

So, we are not required to imagine a single tree with dual trunks arching over the river, but may think of a line of trees on either side of the river, as in Ezekiel 47.

John probably used the singular form in deference to the familiar "tree of life" found in the Garden of Eden and also associated with the source of a river (Gen. 1:9-10).

both food for eating and leaves that bring healing to the nations. While one might think of making herbal poultices from the leaves to bring physical healing, the image is almost certainly metaphorical. In the shade of the trees of life, by the river of life, all who gather there will find whatever healing and health is needed for life. ⛚

In vv. 3-5 we find earlier images repeated. Accursed things are excluded from the Holy City, the throne of God and the lamb are there, and God provides a constant source of light for the city and rules forever.

Of particular interest is the note in v. 4 that, as God's servants offer worship, "they will see his face, and his name will be on their foreheads." The Hebrews believed that anyone who saw God's face would die (Exod. 3:6, 20:19, 33:20-23), and thus that no one had ever seen God (John 1:18, 1 Tim. 6:15).

⛚ **How many kinds of fruit?**
The curious may wonder if Rev. 22:2 means that the trees produced a different type of fruit each month, or if they produced 12 types of fruit together with a new crop each month, or if there is only one type of fruit but the trees produce a new crop each month. The description is not clear enough for a definitive answer: a literal reading would be "producing twelve fruit, according to each month it gives its fruit."

In Ezekiel's vision, which appears to be a pattern for this one, there are various types of fruit trees, producing fruit each month. Thus it is likely that John understands there will be different types of fruit, and that fruit will be available year round. We can't be more specific than that.

In the Holy City, however, believers experience a new intimacy. Standing or kneeling by the river of life and beneath the trees of life, there is no death, and all may finally behold God's face without fear.

That worshipers would have the name of God written on their foreheads recalls Rev. 3:12, 7:1-8, 9:4, and 14:1. Being marked with God's name is a striking way of saying that the inhabitants of the new Jerusalem are truly God's people, living and ruling with God for all time (22:5).

John's vision of the eternal city offers words of both warning and of hope. We are reminded that those who continue to reject God's way have no place there. Since John was writing to Christian people who were facing the temptation to "do as the Romans do" in order to escape persecution, these words would urge them to remain true to their faith, even at the cost of their lives.

At the same time, the glorious future in store for believers—with special attention given to those who are martyred for their faith—could engender courage to stand strong in perilous times.

For Reflection: *Think of how John's apocalyptic message might have encouraged believers who were in danger of persecution or even death if they refused to worship the emperor. Our temptations and struggles are different, but are we any less in need of a similar message in words of both caution and of hope?*

THE HARDEST QUESTION
Will the people of Israel be in heaven?

Revelation 21:10–22:5, with its imagery drawn from both the Old and New Testaments, raises the question of Israel's place in God's future. The term "supersessionism" describes a popular belief that the New Covenant in Christ *supersedes* or replaces the Old Covenant agreement between God and Israel. Thus, in this view, God's covenant with Israel becomes either null or less important, and the Old Testament is largely a lead-up to the New Testament.

Supersessionism comes in a variety of flavors. Some see the New Covenant/Testament as an extension and fulfillment of the Old Covenant/Testament. Others see the new covenant as an addition to the old, while others see the covenant of faith through Christ as a complete replacement of Judaism.

The question has to do with whether God's covenant with Israel has been completely abrogated for Jews who lived before Christ or who do not regard Christ as the messiah, or whether God will redeem Israel based on promises once made to Abraham and his descendants.

Christian theologians have argued for different positions on this topic from the early church fathers until the present, with some holding to a broad view in which there is a place for both Israel and the church in God's future, and others contending that Israel forfeited its place as God's people and is therefore excluded. Other theologians take a variety of positions in between.

To explore this issue in depth would require a much longer discourse than we have space for in this chapter. Suffice it to say that while scriptures can be cited and arguments made in defense of various views, it is one of those questions unlikely to be answered fully in this life. In any case, such matters are best left up to God.

Revelation 22:6-21

I AM COMING SOON!

The Spirit and the bride say, "Come."
And let everyone who hears say, "Come."
And let everyone who is thirsty come.
Let anyone who wishes take the water of life as a gift.
—Revelation 22:17

Have you ever had someone call or text to say they were on their way to meet you, yet you waited and waited, wondering if they would ever really arrive?

We may feel a bit like that in reading this text from Revelation 22. In the epilogue to the book, John quotes Jesus as saying "I am coming soon" no less than three times, and it seems clear that John expected "soon" to mean in the near future, within his lifetime.

Yet, more than 1900 years later, Jesus has not come as John predicted, either for the "rapture" some expect, or for a final judgment. Self-styled prophets have long worked complex calculations based on their preferred interpretation of the symbolic "weeks" in Dan. 9:25, various numbers in Revelation, and signs such as those Jesus is said to have mentioned in the "Little Apocalypse" described in Mark 13, Matthew 24, and Luke 21.

Any number of people through the years have publicly stated a belief that the signs have been fulfilled and Christ will soon return. Various representatives of the Jehovah's Witnesses have done so multiple times during the past century. In the late 1970s Hal Lindsey convinced many people that the end was coming in his best seller, *The Late Great Planet Earth*. In 1988 a former NASA engineer named Edgar Whisenant persuaded backers to finance the cost of printing and mailing thousands of copies of *88 Reasons Why the World Will End in 1988* to pastors across the country, predicting the world would end between Sept. 11 and 13 of that year. He issued updated predictions in 1989, 1993, and 1994. In that same year, evangelist/broadcaster Harold Camping of "Family Radio" convinced many people that the world would end on Sept. 6, 1994. Later predictions included May 21 and Oct. 21, 2011. The year 2015 was marked by assertions from various folk that a fourth "blood moon" would mark the end.

All of these self-styled prophets apparently failed to heed Jesus' own words: "'But about that day and hour no one knows, neither the angels of heaven, nor the Son, but only the Father'" (Mark 13:32, Matt. 24:36). What do we make of this? Should we be expecting Jesus any day now, or not?

AN ANNOUNCEMENT
(vv. 6-11)

We have explained previously that the book of Revelation is primarily an apocalypse, but cast in the form of a letter. As such, it contains a prologue (1:1-8) and an epilogue (22:6-17). These "bookends" share a number of similarities that remind the reader of the book's most important themes. ⚓

The epilogue includes three speakers: Jesus, the angel, and John. Sometimes it is difficult to be sure who is speaking—the early manuscripts did not include punctuation such as quotation marks, so modern translations may differ. ⚓

The "he" who speaks in v. 6 is probably the same angel who had taken John on a tour of the new Jerusalem, assuring him that the words of testimony he had received were "trustworthy and true," and clearly including John in the exalted company of the prophets.

The sudden announcement: "See, I am coming soon!" (v. 7) marks a shift in speaker as Christ takes the floor. It is not an angel's coming, but the return of Jesus that gives hope to John's readers. This is the first of three predictions in the epilogue that Christ will arrive soon (see also vv. 12, 20), though each brings with it a different emphasis. In v. 7, the prediction is followed by a beatitude or

---

⚓ **A helpful inclusio:** Scholars use the term "inclusio" to describe the literary device of beginning and ending a passage with similar "bookends" as a way of uniting what's in the middle and reprising the primary themes. Note the common bonds between John's prologue (1:1-8) and the epilogue (22:6-17):

• a statement that the revelation is from Jesus (1:1; 22:6, 16)
• a testimony to what John saw (1:2, 22:8)
• a blessing on those who read the book and keep its words (1:3; 22:7, 9-10)
• a note that "the time is near" (1:3, 22:10)
• a reference to the churches in Asia (1:4, 22:16)
• a statement that Jesus is coming soon (1:7; 22:7, 12, 20)
• a reference to Jesus/God as the Alpha and Omega (1:8, 22:13)

> 🕎 **Speaking parts:** Mitchell Reddish, in the Smyth & Helwys Commentary on Revelation, assigns the speakers in this text as follows:
>
> - v. 6: angel
> - v. 7: Christ
> - v. 8: John
> - vv. 9-11: angel
> - vv. 12-16: Christ
> - vv. 17-19: John
> - v. 20a: Christ
> - vv. 20b-21: John

blessing on "the one who keeps the words of the prophecy of this book," that is, who pays heed to John's warnings and lives with the courage and hope needed to remain faithful in trying days. 🕎

With v. 8, John himself speaks, testifying that he had indeed seen and heard the things written in the book, vouching for their accuracy. As if to emphasize his honesty in telling "the whole story," he admits to having been reproved by the angel when he fell at his feet as in worship, and was told to worship God alone (v. 9).

This anecdote professes humility on the one hand, but subtly raises John's stature on the other: the angel identified himself as "a fellow servant with you and your comrades the prophets, and with those who keep the words of this book" (v. 9). Thus, John is identified more clearly as belonging among the prophets, but both he and those who followed his teaching were named as "fellow servants" with the mighty angel, in that they all joined in the worship and service of God.

The angel's instructions that John should not seal up the prophecy are in direct contrast to a quite different instruction in the book of Daniel (Dan. 8:26; 12:4, 9). The last six chapters of Daniel almost certainly were

> 🕎 **Beatitudes:** Seven beatitudes are found in the book of Revelation, with the last two occurring in the epilogue:
> 1. "Blessed is the one who reads aloud the words of the prophecy, and blessed are those who hear and who keep what is written in it; for the time is near" (1:3).
> 2. "Blessed are the dead who from now on die in the Lord" (14:13).
> 3. "Blessed is the one who stays awake and is clothed, not going about naked and exposed to shame" (16:15).
> 4. "Blessed are those who are invited to the marriage supper of the Lamb" (19:9).
> 5. "Blessed and holy are those who share in the first resurrection" (20:6).
> 6. "Blessed is the one who keeps the words of the prophecy of this book" (22:7).
> 7. "Blessed are those who wash their robes, so that they will have the right to the tree of life and may enter the city by the gates" (22:14).

written under a pseudonym by an anonymous person in about 170-165 BCE, when the Seleucid ruler Antiochus IV Epiphanes was wreaking havoc upon the Jews and doing his best to eradicate Judaism. The author who encouraged the distressed Jews to persevere wrote as if Daniel had seen the visions nearly 400 years before—insisting that he had been told to "keep the book sealed until the time of the end" (Dan. 12:4). The writer presented his work as the "unsealing" of the ancient prophecies, whose secrets could finally be revealed in his day, which he portrayed as "the time of the end." ♱

In contrast, John openly claimed to be the visionary and author of the book, and wrote as if he truly believed the end was near. Thus, John was compelled to publicize his work as quickly and as widely as possible.

John's words in v. 11—quoting the angel—are a bit of a puzzle. Was John simply to accept that evildoers would remain evil while the righteous remained just? Was it too late for the wicked to repent?

The saying is based on Dan. 12:10, which says that many would be purified, cleansed, or refined, while the wicked would remain firm in their wickedness. Even the statement in Daniel offers little hope of real change: it was the faithful

♱ **Could scripture be misleading?** The analysis provided here—which assumes that the latter half of Daniel was written in the second century but intentionally presented as the work of a prophet named Daniel nearly 400 years before—is commonly accepted by critical scholars, but could prove very challenging to readers who are not familiar with the arguments. Would a biblical author use an intentional artifice to give his writing more weight?

The answer is yes: this was commonly done in the ancient world, and there is no reason to assume that writers whose work made it into the Bible would not follow typical conventions. Of course, none of the ancient authors whose works are found in scripture knew that their work would later be accepted as authoritative scripture.

This is not to say that one cannot hold firm to the belief that a prophet Daniel who lived in the sixth century BCE actually wrote words applicable to the Jews' second-century suffering under Antiochus; that he was instructed to seal it up; that the parchment scroll somehow managed to survive nearly 400 years without being lost, rotting, or turning to dust; and that God inspired a later prophet to find it, unseal it, and proclaim its message.

While that belief remains in the realm of possibility, the scenario of a later writer using the common literary device of writing to present needs but under an ancient hero's name remains the most likely explanation.

Jews who would be purified, cleansed, and refined, while there appears little or no hope that the wicked would change their ways.

Similarly, the angel's words offer little expectation that sinners will be converted by the severe warnings revealed through John's visions. His statement, in fact, is in the imperative mood: let the wicked remain wicked, he seems to say, while the holy remain holy.

Mitchell Reddish suggests that John's intent may be something like this: "Let those who are wicked continue in their wickedness if that is what they choose; but they must pay the consequences. On the other hand, let those who are righteous continue to do what is right because that is what God expects and demands of them."[1]

> **For Reflection:** *Do you think the angel's words in Rev. 22:11 rule out any opportunity for change, either for good or evil? What do you think is the angel's purpose?*

AN INVITATION
(vv. 12-17)

The possibility of change becomes apparent as Jesus speaks again, offering an affirmation of John's testimony, a witness to himself, a blessing upon righteous believers, and a clear invitation for all who wish to come and drink from the water of life.

Christ's second announcement that "I am coming soon" is joined by an affirmation that "my reward is with me, to repay according to everyone's work" (v. 12). This does not suggest a return to a works-righteousness theology. The work of the faithful is to put their faith in Christ and to live accordingly. Believers facing trials were tempted to turn away from their faith, but John insisted that Christ will arrive soon with their recompense in hand.

Jesus' reference to himself as the Alpha and Omega (v. 13) echoes 1:8, where the same term was used as a title for God. This is yet another of Revelation's affirmations that God and Christ are inextricably bound together.

Verse 14 offers a benediction to those who "have washed their robes, so that they will have the right to the tree of life and may enter the city by its gates" (compare 7:14). These are contrasted with those who may not enter the city but remain without: "dogs and sorcerers and fornicators and idolaters, and everyone who loves and practices falsehood" (v. 15, compare similar lists in 21:8 and 17). 🕭

> ⛦ **Left outside:** "Dog" was used as a general term of derision for the wicked, not with reference to a particular sin. Note that the wicked are described as persons who are still actively involved in the particular behaviors listed as examples of evil: sorcery, fornication, murder, idolatry, and deceit. The verse does not suggest that those who have sinned in the past cannot repent and enter the gates to eat from the tree of life, but that those who stubbornly persist in their rebellion must of necessity remain outside.

With vv. 16-17, we come to some of the most memorable words in John's remarkable book. Jesus affirms again that he is responsible for the message, and identifies himself as "the root and the descendant of David, the bright morning star" (v. 16).

The first title draws on Isaiah's prediction of a coming one as both a shoot and a root from the stump of Jesse, David's father (Isa. 11:1, 10). This prediction came to be understood in messianic terms. Thus, for Jesus to claim the title "son of David" was to acknowledge his identity as the messiah.

Jesus' self-description as "the bright morning star," which may have some root in Num. 24:17, is not found elsewhere in the New Testament, though Jesus elsewhere refers to himself as the light of the world. ⛦

In v. 17 we find the beautiful, repetitive words of invitation that make Revelation a book of bright hope as well as dire warning:

The Spirit and the bride say, "Come."
And let everyone who hears say, "Come."
And let everyone who is thirsty come.
Let anyone who wishes take the water of life as a gift.

The first two lines may be understood as a call for Christ to "come" in the sense of the second coming, or as the first part of an invitation that clearly concludes with an opportunity for all to choose life.

> ⛦ **Son of a star:** The prediction from Numbers that "a star shall come out of Jacob and a scepter shall rise out of Israel" was also understood in messianic terms, and at least one revolutionary who thought of himself as the messiah adopted it: a man named Simon bar Kosiba, who led an ill-fated revolt against the Romans in 132-35 CE, went by the moniker "*Bar Kokhba,*" meaning "Son of the Star."

John sees a time when Christ's work is done, the gates of heaven are opened, and "anyone who wishes" may come and "take the water of life as a gift."

The beauty and simplicity of the invitation do not obviate the importance of repentance and faith, but firmly focus on the universal availability of salvation to those who thirst for it, who come for it, and who receive it as a gift.

Thanks be to God.

> **For Reflection:** *How does the repetitive language of 22:17 amplify or emphasize the expansive grace of God? Have you come to accept God's gift?*

A WARNING
(vv. 18-21)

The last few verses bring a change in tone as the author pronounces a curse upon anyone who adds to or takes away from what he has written (vv. 18-19). This was not an uncommon practice, and its intention was obvious: to maintain the book as John wrote it, without change.

People in the ancient world took curses seriously. Tomb inscriptions often concluded with a curse directed at anyone who disturbed the bones of the diseased, and with some important documents, official ceremonies placing a curse on violators might be held. ♙

♙ **Laying a curse:** For the ancients, cursing was far more than obscene or disrespectful language. Curses called upon the deity to bring specific troubles upon any who violated a certain prohibition.

A notable example is found in the famous Letter of Aristeas, which makes rather unbelievable claims about how 72 different scholars in Alexandria each translated the Hebrew Scriptures into Greek—perfectly. As an assembly of priests heard the newly translated books read, the letter said, certain leaders of the people said: "Since this version has been made rightly and reverently, and in every respect accurately, it is good that this should remain exactly so, and that there should be no revision."

"There was general approval of what they said," Aristeas reported, "and they commanded that a curse should be laid, as was their custom, on anyone who should alter the version by any addition or change to any part of the written text, or any deletion either. This was a good step taken to ensure that the words were preserved completely and permanently in perpetuity."[2]

Following the curse, John returns to a more positive conclusion, again affirming that his words are directly from Christ, who asserts, for the third time, "Surely I am coming soon" (v. 20a).

John responds with an exclamation, "Amen. Come Lord Jesus!" John indicates that he is ready, willing, and hopeful that Christ will indeed come, and come soon.

How should modern believers respond to John's book of Revelation? We do not live in the same sort of desperate times that plagued John's hearers. And, we must acknowledge that John's predictions of Jesus' quick return did not materialize. Does this mean that John's book is not useful for believers of today?

Contemporary Christians misuse the book of Revelation if we dwell too much on its apocalyptic predictions, anticipate a literal fulfillment of John's metaphorical images, try to construct a timetable for Jesus' return, or draw building plans for the new Jerusalem. That was not John's intent.

We can, however, find in John's word-pictures beautiful images of the Christian hope: that we can rest secure in the power of God and the Lamb to rule the universe and redeem those who hear and follow the call to trust and faithful discipleship. Surely we can join John in saying "Amen" to that.

For Reflection: *How did you feel about the book of Revelation before undertaking this study, and how did you think it should be interpreted? Has your understanding of Revelation changed as a result of this study? If so, how?*

THE HARDEST QUESTION
Does Revelation 22:17 teach universal salvation?

Readers of Rev. 22:6-21 will run across several interpretive puzzles, including the question of whether John believed in universal salvation. While of great interest, answering that question would require many words in order to conclude that we cannot give a definitive answer: there are verses in Revelation that point toward a belief that all will be saved, and other verses that suggest a clear belief that those who persist in rebellion against God will be excluded.

Of particular interest is the interpretation of 22:17, which declares the good news that the water of life is available to all who thirst and who seek it. But what, precisely, is happening in this verse?

I suspect that most readers take all four lines of the poetic verse as a repetitive invitation to humans in need of the water of life. Several commentators argue, however, that the first two lines are a call for Christ—who has promised "I am coming soon"—to come and fulfill his work. This interpretation is strengthened in that it is the Spirit and the bride (the church) who offer the first invitation, and "everyone who hears" who repeat it. In both cases, the imperative verb translated as "Come" is singular.

This observation is not conclusive, however. The next two lines, clearly directed to "everyone who is thirsty" and "anyone who wishes to take the water of life" also employ singular verbs because the words translated as "anyone" and "everyone" are collective nouns that take a singular verb. The verbs do shift from second person to third-person, but all are in the imperative form and can be interpreted as an invitation.

Whether the string of invitations applies first for Christ to come and then to those who need to receive the water of life that Christ offers; or whether it refers to those who thirst for the water of life throughout, the end result is the same: life with God is available to all who will seek it.

Revelation 22:17 reflects a similar invitation in Isa. 55:1: "Ho, everyone who thirsts, come to the waters; and you that have no money, come, buy and eat! Come, buy wine and milk without money and without price."

Life—both in the present and the potential for eternal life—is a gift from God and available to all. To this good news of grace we may conclude with John: "The grace of the Lord Jesus Christ be with all the saints. Amen."

NOTES

[1]Mitchell G. Reddish, *Revelation*, Smyth & Helwys Commentary (Macon, GA: Smyth & Helwys, 2001), 426.

[2]From the "Letter of Aristeas," trans. R.J.H. Shutt, in *The Old Testament Pseudepigraha*, ed, James H. Charlesworth, 2 vols. (New York: Doubleday & Co., 1985), 2:33; cited by Reddish in *Revelation*, 430.

AFTERWORD

I n the book of Revelation we find a collection of puzzling and occasionally bizarre visions that have attracted some readers and repelled others from the time of its first circulation among the churches of Asia Minor.

In this book of studies from selected texts in Revelation, we have argued that we need not be afraid of the book, or overly enamored with it—but we should acquire the appropriate interpretive tools with which to read it.

As an apocalypse, Revelation was written during a period of great trial when individuals and churches alike suffered under the heavy hand of Roman oppression, particularly with respect to the imperial cult that demanded all residents to pay homage to the emperor. Some Christians bravely died for their faith, while others abandoned it. To encourage believers in Asia and elsewhere, John wrote to share his belief that Christ would return soon to defeat and banish all that is evil, and then to create a new heaven and a new earth where the faithful could dwell in the peace and presence of God forever.

Our studies have taken a close look at some of the images John used, understanding them as the metaphors they were designed to be, rather than a literal description or timeline predicting an end-times scenario.

John's imagery focuses on the power and patience of God, the person of Christ, the persistence of evil, and the promise that God and good will prevail. In reading the account of John's extraordinary visions, we must exercise holy imagination and spiritual discernment as we seek to apply lessons designed for a different time to our own situations in life. Doing so will not turn us into prophets or answer all of our questions, but a careful reading of Revelation brings not only a clear challenge to faithfulness in adversity, but also the comforting testimony that God reigns, that evil will end, and that hope endures.

What more could we ask?

www.ingramcontent.com/pod-product-compliance
Lightning Source LLC
Chambersburg PA
CBHW060425090426
42734CB00011B/2455